# HOMO SAPIENS PART - IX

## SIXTY ODES TO HUMANITY: A COLLECTION OF POETIC REFLECTIONS

### MAWPHNIANG NAPOLEON

To all valued readers, I dedicate this verse,
With examples from literature that I implore,
To show my gratitude for your interest,
In this book and its series that you implore,
And to inspire you to read and verse,
For the love of words, in this literary store.

In this literary store, I invite you to delve,
Into the pages of this book and its series,
And discover the wonders of written verse,
The power of words that make our hearts implore,
And the emotions that literature can serve,
For all valued readers, this gift I implore.

From Shakespeare's sonnets to Milton's epic verse,
The classics of literature offer us more,
Than just words on paper, but life to implore,
And lessons to learn, in this literary store,
For all valued readers, I ask that you traverse,
The depths of this book and its series.

In this book and its series, I offer my verse,
Inspired by the greats, to those who implore,
The beauty of words and their meaning, to preserve,
And continue the legacy of literature, to serve,
All valued readers, with a passion to immerse,
In this literary store, a treasure trove.

So to all valued readers, I dedicate this verse,

With examples from literature, to implore,

Your love of words and this book's series, to traverse,

And explore the endless possibilities, to preserve,

The magic of words, in this literary store,

For the love of literature, I serve.


And in this literary store, I shall serve,

To all valued readers, with this verse,

For the love of literature, I implore,

And the passion for words, to preserve,

This book and its series, for all to traverse,

And discover the beauty of written words.


From Author

# Contents

# Contents

# Contents

# Contents

# Foreword

From the depth of human experience and the breadth of our collective consciousness, comes a symphony of words that resonate with the essence of our being. Mawphniang Napoleon's 'Homo Sapiens Part – IX, Sixty Odes to Humanity' is a collection of poetic reflections that explore the many facets of our existence, from the sweet melodies of love to the dark plights of fate and the burden of secrets. This book invites us to contemplate the timeless questions of our existence and the beauty of life, seen through the lens of sixty poems that are both introspective and universal. As we turn each page, we are taken on a journey of self-discovery and realization, transported by the lyrical luminescence of Shillong and the enigma of the self. This is a tribute to the legacy of humanity and a celebration of our eternal splendor. Let us embrace this musical ode to life and bask in the light of its timeless wisdom."

Special Regards ,

A - Team

# Preface

"Beneath the veil of life's complexities, lies a timeless essence that speaks to the soul. In this book, 'Homo Sapiens Part – IX, Sixty Odes to Humanity: A Collection of Poetic Reflections,' Mawphniang Napoleon takes us on a journey through the depths of humanity's emotions, thoughts, and experiences. With each poem, we are invited to reflect upon the beauty, darkness, and mystery of the human experience. From the sweet-voiced seraph of Pipa to the timeless lament of the bibliophile, these sixty odes offer a musical tapestry of humanity's intricacies and passions. Let these poetic reflections be your guide as you explore the depths of the human spirit."

Special Regards ,

A - Team

# Acknowledgements

Dear Readers,

It is with great humility and gratitude that I take this opportunity to acknowledge the countless individuals who have contributed to the creation of this book.

To my family, who has supported me through thick and thin, and who has always encouraged me to pursue my passions, thank you for always being there for me.

To my friends, who have been my confidants, my sounding boards, and my cheerleaders, thank you for your unwavering support and encouragement.

To the countless individuals who have been my muses, who have inspired me to capture their stories in verse, thank you for allowing me to delve into the depths of your souls.

Finally, to you, dear readers, thank you for giving this book a chance. Thank you for taking the time to read these poems and for allowing me to share my thoughts and experiences with you.

This book is a testament to the power of the human spirit, to the beauty of the human experience, and to the resilience of the human heart. I hope that you find something in these pages that speaks to you, that touches your soul, and that leaves a lasting impression on your heart.

With gratitude and love,

Warm regards ,

Mawphniang Napoleon

Syadheh , Ri Bhoi District

Meghalaya

# Prologue

Ladies and Gentlemen, we invite you to embark on a journey of self-discovery, a journey into the depths of the human soul. A journey that will take you through the many facets of humanity, its beauty and its flaws, its sorrows and its joys. In this book, "Homo Sapiens Part – IX, Sixty Odes to Humanity: A Collection of Poetic Reflections," Mawphniang Napoleon invites you to experience the world through his eyes, to feel the emotions that he has captured in verse.

As you turn the pages of this book, you will encounter poems that will transport you to different realms, poems that will make you question the very essence of existence. You will be moved by the beauty of the sweet-voiced Seraph of Pipa, mesmerized by the timeless melody of the Duitara and awed by the lyrical luminescence of Shillong. You will be forced to confront the complexities of fate and destiny, to ponder the enigma of self, to confront the legacy of Likai and to celebrate the leaf of equality.

This book is not just a collection of poems, it is a collection of moments, of memories, of thoughts, and of experiences that have been captured in verse. It is an invitation to explore the uncharted territories of the human heart and to connect with the human experience in a way that words alone cannot.

So dear readers, we invite you to sit back, relax and let the poetry of Mawphniang Napoleon take you on a journey that you will never forget. A journey that will leave you with a renewed appreciation for the beauty and wonder of humanity.

Special Regards ,

A - Team

# 1. Oh Pippa, Sweet-Voiced Seraph

Oh fair Pippa, sweet and fair of face,
Thy voice doth sing of love and mirth,
Of dreams and wishes, of life's sweet grace,
And all the beauty that doth give birth.

The sun doth rise in orient's glow,
And sets in occident with its feast,
The moon doth shine in starry show,
And stars doth twinkle in the east.

The flowers doth bloom in spring's fair light,
And leaves doth fall in autumn's chill,
The birds doth sing in summer's bright,
And snowflakes fall in winter's still.

The oceans wild, the rivers free,
The mountains high, the skies so blue,
The rainbows bright, the sunshine be,
All beauty that surroundseth me and you.

So sing, sweet Pippa, sing to me,
Thy song doth soothe my soul and fill my heart with glee.

Thy melody doth lift my spirits high,

And fill my mind with thoughts of hope,
Of all the joys that life doth supply,
And all the beauty that doth elope.

In youth and age, thy song doth ring,
Of all the dreams that we pursue,
The laughter and the tears we bring,
All part of life's great tapestry, true.

The struggles we must oft endure,
The battles we must fight each day,
The determination to be sure,
And resilience that doth make us sway.

So sing, sweet Pippa, sing to me,
Thy song doth guide my steps and set my heart aglow,
For in thy melody, I see,
The beauty of life that's yet to know.

Thy verse doth paint a picture bright,
Of all the wonders we behold,
The magic in the morning light,
And the secrets that stories told.

The beauty in the ordinary,
The magic in the simple things,
The hope that guides us on our journey,
And the love that makes our hearts sing.

So sing, sweet Pippa, sing to me,
Thy song doth echo through the ages,
A symphony of life and destiny,
A treasure that forever sages.

Thy voice doth soar like a sweet bird,
And fill my heart with pure delight,
For in thy song, I have heard,
The beauty of life shining bright.

Thy melody doth resonate deep,
In every corner of my mind,
A symphony of joy and sleep,
A harmony that's hard to find.

A reminder of the beauty that surrounds us,
A celebration of life's simple things,
A reflection of the love that astound us,
And the hope that makes our hearts sing.

So sing, sweet Pippa, sing to me,
Thy song doth fill my heart with wonder,
A symphony of life and destiny,
A treasure that will never sunder.

For in thy voice, I find my peace,
And in thy song, my heart finds release.

Thy melody doth take me away,

To far-off lands and distant skies,
A journey through life's winding way,
With beauty that forever lies.

In every verse, a new tale unfolds,
Of love and laughter, of hope and dreams,
Of stories yet to be told,
And memories yet to be gleaned.

So sing, sweet Pippa, sing to me,
Thy song doth weave a magic spell,
A symphony of life and destiny,
A story that forever dwells.

For in thy song, I find my way,
And in thy melody, I hear my fate say.

Thy song is like a melody of the heart,
A symphony of joy and sorrow,
A reflection of life's every part,
A tale for every tomorrow.

It speaks of love that knows no bounds,
And of laughter that echoes through the years,
Of hope that surrounds us all around,
And of beauty that never disappears.

So sing, sweet Pippa, sing to me,
Thy song is a treasure to behold,

A symphony of life and destiny,
A story that forever will be told.

For in thy voice, I find my way,
And in thy melody, I hear my fate say.

Sing on, sweet Pippa, sing on,
For your song is a symphony of life,
A melody that will forever be strong,
A treasure that will never lose its shine.

Thy song doth echo through the ages,
A symphony of love and light,
A reflection of life's many stages,
A beacon shining bright.

It speaks of the joys and sorrows,
Of the laughter and the tears,
Of the beauty and the morrows,
Of the hopes and fears.

So sing, sweet Pippa, sing to me,
Thy song doth fill my heart with hope,
A symphony of life and destiny,
A treasure that will help me cope.

For in thy voice, I find my strength,
And in thy melody, I find my length.

Sing on, sweet Pippa, sing on,
For your song is a symphony of life,
A melody that will forever be strong,
A treasure that will never lose its shine.

# 2. The Soul of the Mountains: The Duitara's Timeless Melody

In the mountains of Meghalaya, a sound doth resound,
From a four-stringed instrument, named Ka Duitara, renowned.
A folk musical instrument, its beauty doth astound,
Its body strong and sturdy, of hard wood it is bound.
A hollow in its belly, coated with dried animal skin,
And in its neck, four holes, in which wooden pegs spin.

Its strings of muga silk, doth create a wondrous strain,
That lifts the soul, and fills the heart with joy and gain.
Unlike the bow-shaped veena, santoor, ektara, tambura, jantra,
The duitara's melody, doth shine brighter, like the North Star.
Sarod and sarangi, it hath not, for it is unique,
A treasure of the Khasi and Jaintia folks, its mystique.

The term duitara, similar to the dotara of Assam and Bengal,
Doth evoke memories of a time, when life was simple and plain.
A time when music was a means, to communicate and express,
The joys and sorrows, of a people, who lived life nonetheless.

And yet, the duitara doth endure, its music still doth soar,
A symbol of the culture, of the Khasi and Jaintia folks.
For in its strings, a history doth lie, of a people's past,

A tale of struggles, and triumphs, that will forever last.

So, let us raise our voices, in tribute to the duitara's sound,
For it is a reminder, of a people's rich cultural ground.
And let us cherish, the music that it doth create,
For it is a reflection, of a people's love, and their fate.

For in the duitara, a mystery doth lie,
A mystery that only the mountains, and its music, can deny.
A mystery that doth enrapture, and doth captivate,
A mystery that will forever, be part of the Khasi and Jaintia state.

And as the strings doth play, a spell it doth cast,
A spell that doth transport, us to a world of the past.
A world of tradition, and a world of old,
A world where music was, the heart and soul.

And yet, the duitara doth endure, and its music doth persist,
A testament to a people's heritage, and their musical bliss.
For in its notes, a history doth sing, of a people's plight,
And in its rhythm, a legacy doth live, of a people's might.

So let us listen, to the duitara's sweet, melodic song,
For it doth embody, the spirit, of a people so strong.
And let us pay homage, to the musicians who play,
For they are the keepers, of a tradition, that will never fade away.

For in the duitara, a spirit doth reside,
A spirit that doth uplift, and never doth subside.

A spirit that doth connect, us to our roots,
A spirit that doth inspire, and enlighten our boots.

And as the duitara doth play, a tale it doth unfold,
A tale of a people's culture, that doth never grow old.
A tale of love and laughter, and a tale of tears,
A tale that doth touch, our hearts, and calm our fears.

So, let us cherish, the duitara and its music so grand,
For it is a treasure, that doth grace our land.
A treasure that doth celebrate, our cultural roots,
A treasure that doth bring, us closer, to our fruits.

And let us remember, the duitara's timeless song,
For it is a symbol, of a people's history, so long.
And let us honor, the musicians who play,
For they are the guardians, of a tradition, that will always stay.

For in the duitara's melody, a story doth unfold,
A story of a people, their struggles, and their hold.
A story of resilience, and a story of hope,
A story that doth inspire, and give us strength to cope.

And as we listen, to the duitara's soothing sound,
We are reminded, of a people's rich cultural ground.
And we are filled, with a sense of pride,
For we are part, of a heritage, so bright and wide.

So let us cherish, the duitara and its music so dear,

For it is a part, of our cultural legacy, so clear.
And let us keep alive, the tradition that it brings,
For it is a gift, that forever, our spirits will sing.

For the duitara, is more than just an instrument to play,
It is a symbol, of a people's cultural way.
It is a reminder, of our roots, and our past,
A reminder, that will forever, our hearts will last.

And as we bask, in the duitara's sweet and soothing sound,
We are taken back, to a world, where music, was so profound.
A world, where songs were sung, and tales were told,
A world, where music, was the life and soul.

And as the duitara sings, its tales of old,
We are transported, to a place, where legends unfold.
Where heroes were born, and myths were made,
Where music was the magic, that never faded.

And as the duitara strums, its strings so fine,
We are captivated, by its melodies so divine.
For in its music, a mystery doth reside,
A mystery that forever, will never subside.

So let us cherish, the duitara and its music so rare,
For it is a part, of our cultural heritage so fair.
And let us keep alive, the tradition that it brings,
For it is a gift, that forever, our spirits will sing.

For the duitara, is a treasure, that doth shine,
A treasure, that will forever, be forever thine.
So, let us listen, to its music, with care and grace,
And let us keep alive, its tradition, with love and pace.

And as the duitara's notes, fill the air so clear,
We are transported, to a world, without any fear.
A world, where music, is the bridge between our hearts,
A world, where peace, and love, forever, it imparts.

For in the duitara's sounds, we find a solace so sweet,
A solace, that lifts our souls, and sets our worries free.
And as we listen, to its melodies so pure and true,
We are reminded, of a people's heritage, that shines so bright and new.

And so let us celebrate, the duitara and its music so grand,
For it is a gift, that forever, our hearts will command.
And let us honor, the musicians who play,
For they are the keepers, of a tradition, that will always stay.

For the duitara, is more than just a musical instrument,
It is a symbol, of a people's culture, so intrinsic and content.
And as we listen, to its music, we are filled with pride,
For we are part, of a heritage, that will never subside.

So let us cherish, the duitara and its music so dear,
For it is a part, of our cultural legacy, so clear.
And let us keep alive, the tradition that it brings,
For it is a gift, that forever, our spirits will sing.

And as the duitara strums, its strings so fine and true,
We are reminded, of a time, when music was pure and new.
A time, when songs were sung, with love and care,
A time, when music, was the light that shone so fair.

For in the duitara's music, we find a truth so bright,
A truth, that shines so strong, and shines with all its might.
And as we listen, to its melodies so pure and sweet,
We are filled with hope, and our souls are lifted off our feet.

And so let us keep alive, the duitara and its music so rare,
For it is a part, of a heritage, that we should all share.
And let us honor, the musicians who play,
For they are the keepers, of a tradition, that will always stay.

For the duitara, is more than just an instrument to play,
It is a symbol, of a people's cultural way.
It is a reminder, of our roots, and our past,
A reminder, that will forever, our hearts will last.

So let us cherish, the duitara and its music so dear,
For it is a part, of our cultural legacy, so clear.
And let us keep alive, the tradition that it brings,
For it is a gift, that forever, our spirits will sing.

# 3. Shillong's Lyrical Luminescence

In the city light of Shillong,
A metropolis of vibrant throngs,
A bustling hub of human toil,
Where the hustle and bustle never boils.

But as I gaze upon its gleam,
I cannot help but ponder and dream,
Of the parallels between its spark,
And the essence of life's eternal arc.

For just as the city never sleeps,
Life too, is a ceaseless journey that creeps,
With each day bringing new endeavors,
And each night, new dreams to treasure.

Just as the city is built on a foundation,
Life too, is constructed on a sensation,
Of growth, adaptation, and evolution,
Ever-changing, yet with a steadfast solution.

And just as the city is a melting pot,
Life too, is a diverse, multicultural lot,
With each individual a unique creation,
Bringing forth their own inspiration.

But as the city's light fades with dawn,
And its inhabitants move on,
So too must we, in life, eventually depart,
Leaving behind our own unique imprint on the heart.

Thus, in the city light of Shillong,
I find solace in this profound song,
That life, like the city, is a fleeting thing,
But its essence, forever, shall sing.

But as I ponder on the city's fate,
I cannot help but contemplate,
The fragility of our existence,
And the transience of our persistence.

For just as the city may rise and fall,
Life too, is subject to nature's call,
With its beauty and grandeur,
Forever fleeting, like a summer's flower.

And just as the city's light may dim,
Life too, is subject to the whims,
Of fate and destiny, and all that be,
Leaving us to wonder, what is meant to be.

But in the midst of all this chaos,
There lies a glimmer of hope and auspicious,
For just as the city may rebuild and renew,

Life too, holds the potential to start anew.

And as the city's lights twinkle and shine,
I am reminded of the human mind,
That is capable of creating and building,
And of the infinite possibilities for yielding.

For just as the city is a work of art,
Life too, is a masterpiece in its own part,
With each person a unique brush stroke,
Leaving their mark on the world's canvas, to provoke.

And just as the city's lights guide us in the night,
Life too, can be a guiding light,
Showing us the way through the dark,
And leading us to our own unique spark.

But as the city's lights fade in the dawn,
And the hustle and bustle is gone,
We must remember that life is fleeting,
But the memories we make will forever be greeting.

And as the city's lights flicker and dance,
I am reminded of the human chance,
To make a difference, to leave a mark,
To strive for greatness, and leave our own spark.

For just as the city is a work in progress,
Life too, is a journey, an endless quest,

With each step an opportunity to grow,
To explore, to create, to let our spirits flow.

And just as the city's lights reflect our hopes,
Life too, is a mirror of our own scope,
Of our fears, our dreams, our aspirations,
And the path we choose to take, in our own station.

But as the city's lights fade in the dawn,
And the hustle and bustle is gone,
We must remember that life is fleeting,
But the memories we make will forever be fleeting.

And as the city's lights shine bright,
I am reminded of the human insight,
To see beyond the surface, to delve deep,
To find meaning, to seek truth, to keep.

For just as the city is more than what it seems,
Life too, holds secrets and hidden themes,
With each layer revealing something new,
A complexity, a mystery, a puzzle to pursue.

And just as the city's lights illuminate the night,
Life too, can bring clarity, a guiding light,
Showing us the way to our true selves,
And the path to our own inner wealths.

But as the city's lights fade in the dawn,

And the hustle and bustle is gone,
We must remember that life is fleeting,
But the memories we make will forever be fleeting.

And as the city's lights blaze and glow,
I am reminded of the human flow,
Of emotions and thoughts, and of our inner strife,
Of the struggles we face in our journey of life.

For just as the city is a place of contrasts,
Life too, is a dichotomy, at times, aghast,
With moments of joy and moments of pain,
Of sunshine and rain, and a love that wanes.

And just as the city's lights flicker and flit,
Life too, is a journey with its own twists and turns,
With each bend bringing new challenges,
And new opportunities to learn.

But as the city's lights fade in the dawn,
And the hustle and bustle is gone,
We must remember that life is fleeting,
But the memories we make will forever be fleeting.

And as the city's lights shine so bright,
I am reminded of the human plight,
To seek out knowledge, to explore the unknown,
And to push the boundaries of what we've known.

For just as the city is a place of innovation,
Life too, is a journey of exploration,
With each step a chance to learn and grow,
To push the limits and reach for the next flow.

And just as the city's lights reach for the sky,
Life too, is an opportunity to soar high,
To reach for our dreams and aspirations,
And to make a difference in the world's equation.

But as the city's lights fade in the dawn,
And the hustle and bustle is gone,
We must remember that life is fleeting,
But the memories we make will forever be fleeting.

So let us embrace the city's light,
And all it represents in our plight,
For it serves as a reminder, a metaphor,
Of the beauty and fleetingness of life, forevermore.

# 4. Eternality's Illusion: A Midnight Musing on Fate and Destiny

Upon a midnight dreary, thoughts of fate and destiny,

Whispered through my mind with eerie, questions of reality.

Do we truly hold the power, to shape our own fate's path,

Or are we but mere puppets, controlled by fate's aftermath.


Illusions of control, do they truly exist,

Or are they but a mirage, in this world of mist.

For in this world of suffering, true freedom is but a myth,

And all that awaits us, is the void of eternal abyss.


Are the choices we make, truly our own,

Or are they predetermined, by fate's unknown.

And what is the point, of striving to be free,

When all that awaits us, is the void of eternity.


So let us not delude ourselves, with the idea of control,

For in the grand scheme of things, we are but mere mortals, whole.

And as we journey through this world, let us not forget,

That in the end, it is all for naught, our fate already set.


Do we truly have a choice, in the face of despair,

Or is it all predetermined, by fate's silent repair.

And in this world of pain and sorrow, is there a truth to find,
Or is it all but a mirage, in the mind.

So let us embrace the darkness, let us accept our fate,
And in the face of suffering, let us remain steadfast and great.
But in the end, what is the point, of striving to be free,
When all that awaits us, is the void of eternity.

Do we truly hold the power, to shape our own destiny,
Or are we but mere puppets, controlled by fate's infinity.
And in the end, what is the point, of seeking solace there,
When all that awaits us, is the void of eternal air.

Is freedom but a dream, in this world of pain,
Or is it a reality, that we can attain.
And in the end, what is the point, of embracing the dark,
When there might be a light, at the end of the arc.

Questions of fate and destiny, do they truly exist,
Or are they but illusions, in the mind's mist.
For in this world of suffering, what is the ultimate truth,
And what is the point, of seeking the proof.

So let us not be fooled, by illusions of control,
For in this world of suffering, true freedom is but a scroll.
And in the end, what is the point, of striving to be free,
When all that awaits us, is the void of eternity.

But perhaps there is more, to this world of pain and strife,

Perhaps there is a purpose, beyond this mortal life.
Perhaps there is a glimmer, of hope in the dark,
A chance to break free, from fate's eternal mark.

For if we truly believe, that our fate is not set,
We can strive to change it, with every step and every breath.
We can seek to break free, from fate's cruel chains,
And in the end, find true freedom, in the eternal rains.

But perhaps, it is not about freedom, or control,
Perhaps it is about the journey, and the stories it holds.
Perhaps it is about the choices we make, and the paths we tread,
The memories we create, and the love that we spread.

For in this world of suffering, true freedom may be a myth,
But perhaps, it is not about freedom, but the beauty in the abyss.
For in the end, it is not the destination, but the journey we make,
That makes our existence, worth the pain and the ache.

So let us not despair, in the face of fate's cruel hand,
Let us not give up, on the journey we have planned.
For in this world of suffering, true freedom may be a dream,
But perhaps, it is not about freedom, but the beauty in the scheme.

But even as we strive, to break free from fate's hold,
We must remember, that we are but mere mortals, old.
For even as we seek, to shape our own destiny,
We must accept, that we are but mere mortals, you and me.

And as we journey through this world, with all its pain and strife,
We must remember, that our time is fleeting, like the flicker of life.
For in the end, it is not about freedom, or control,
But about the journey, and the memories we hold.

So let us not despair, in the face of fate's cruel hand,
Let us not give up, on the journey we have planned.
For in this world of suffering, true freedom may be a dream,
But perhaps, it is not about freedom, but the beauty in the scheme.

And as we journey through this world, with all its pain and strife,
Let us remember, that our time is fleeting, like the flicker of life.
Let us not waste our time, on illusions of control,
But instead embrace the journey, and the memories that unfold.

For in the end, it is not about freedom, or control,
But about the journey, and the memories that we hold.
So let us embrace the journey, and accept our fate,
For in the end, it is all a part of life's great debate.

# 5. Ode to Iewduh

Verily, in Motphran, there doth reside
A market, steeped in tradition, grand and wide,
A labyrinthine maze, where commerce doth thrive,
And cultural riches, to the world, do bide.

This market, one of the largest in the land,
Is guarded by the Khasi chieftains, wise and grand,
A bastion of the people's livelihood, a hallowed space,
That showcases the essence of the state's time-worn race.

The market is divided into sections rare,
Each area, dedicated to a specific wares,
From traditional delicacies, to items oft sought,
To fruits and vegetables, from the earth, wrought.

It is a place not for the light-hearted, truly,
With narrow lanes, and crowds that swirl, free and fleet,
But fear not, for there's always a path to be found,
With many exit points, to lead one safely out of the town.

To explore the state through its core, 'tis wise,
To visit Iewduh, this market of great prize,
For here, one can discover the essence of the land,
And the heritage, that doth forever stand.

The market, it is a place of mystery,
Of secrets and stories, of great diversity,
A testament to the people's resilience, their strength,
Their source of livelihood, a triumph at length.

And so, as the days pass by, and the market doth thrive,
Let us not forget its importance, as we keep our eyes alive,
To the cultural and traditional riches, it doth hold,
And to the people, who it does, forever uphold.

Verily, in Iewduh, the market doth reside,
A place of commerce, tradition, and cultural pride,
A labyrinthine maze, where the spirit of the land doth shine,
A place not for the light-hearted, but for those who seek to refine.

The market of Motphran, an enigma most profound,
A labyrinth of lanes, so labyrinthine, it surrounds,
The heart of the Khasi people, their source of livelihood,
Their legacy and traditions, so timeless, so prized,
Their livelihood, their culture, their existence,
All intertwined in this market's immense persistence.

The vendors cry out their wares, a symphony so rare,
Their voices, like a chorus, so rich, so full of air,
Their offerings a bounty, a feast for the eyes,
Each corner, a treasure trove, of goods, so surprising,
The colors, the textures, the fragrances, all so bright,
A celebration of life, a symbol of the Khasi's might.

The aisles are filled with crowds, their feet pounding the ground,
Their steps, like a drum beat, resounding, all around,
Their hands, reaching for goods, a dance so elegant,
The jostling and the pushing, a chaotic symphony, a hint,
Of the beauty that lies within, in this market of wealth,
A place, where the Khasi's culture, their existence, it delves.

And within the market's heart, the Khasi chieftains hold court,
Their wisdom, their judgment, a guiding light, in this vault,
Of tradition and culture, of goods and services, so grand,
Their presence, a symbol, of the Khasi's noble stand,
Their rule, just and fair, their leadership, so revered,
The market of Motphran, a source of strength, so clear.

The market, a microcosm, of the Khasi's way of life,
Their customs, their traditions, their beliefs, without strife,
Their way of living, a lesson, for the world to see,
The value of community, of unity, and diversity,
The market of Motphran, a window to the Khasi's soul,
A place, where their existence, their culture, doth unfold.

And as the market day draws to a close, the crowds do retire,
The vendors, their goods, do pack, to then again aspire,
To another day, another chance, to serve their people, so dear,
The market, its lanes, its aisles, no longer filled with cheer,
But the memories linger, of the Khasi's livelihood,
Their existence, their culture, in this market, intertwined.

The market of Motphran, a testament to time,

Its legacy, its traditions, so sublime,
A source of livelihood, for the Khasi's, so proud,
A place, where their existence, their culture, does shout loud,
The message of their people, their way of life, so true,
The market of Motphran, a symbol of the Khasi's virtue.

In the heart of Motphran, the local market stands,
An exhibit of the source of livelihood's hand,
Of the people of the state, the Khasi's proud land.
Its ancient halls, a testament to time's command,
And its large sections, a testament to the planned,
Division of the market, for each purpose grand.

For there, in the market's heart, one may be found,
Lost in the maze of its bustling market's sound,
But not without a way to escape, for there's always a way out bound,
By the many exit and entry points that have been unbound,
By the Khasi chieftains, who keep watch around,
The market's many sections, each purpose unbound.

For each area, dedicated to a specific possession or ingredient,
The market is a treasure trove of the state's inherent,
Flavors, colors, and scents, that are never absent,
And one may find there, a traditional Khasi delicacy sent,
Or an item or article used by the locals that is meant,
To showcase the culture and traditions that are never bent.

It is a place where science and philosophy entwine,
For it is here, in the market's heart, that the secrets are confined,

And the enigma of the state's existence is redefined,
Through the hustling and bustling of the daily grind,
And the exchange of goods and services that are aligned,
With the source of livelihood that is unrefined.

It is a place where one may explore the state's core,
Where the essence of the Khasi's heart, forever more,
Is imbued in every item and article sold,
And the stories behind them, forever untold,
Are woven into the fabric of the market's hold,
An inspiration for those who would venture and explore.

And so, in the market's heart, the sestina ends,
But not without a testament to the market's many bends,
And the secrets and enigmas it holds and tends,
For it is here, in Motphran, that the state's legacy extends,
And the Khasi's proud heritage, forever ascends,
In the heart of the local market, its story never bends.

# 6. Melancholy in the crowded streets of New Delhi : An Ode to Longing

In the New Delhi's crowded streets, where filth and grime do reign,
A lawyer's mind doth yearn for fields of green and gold,
For life as free as a farmer in the Ri-Bhoi valley,
Where neighbours are like family, bonds of love untold.

But here in this metropolis, where all is cold and strange,
I know not those who dwell beside me, though I try
To reach out in friendship, yet a gap doth still remain,
Of unfriendliness and unwelcoming, a silent sigh.

For in this city, I cannot walk with ease and grace,
As I might in the village, by the river streams,
For exercise doth bring me only fear and stress,
In a gym, where time and security doth seem.

By night, my friends do call for whiskey, beer, and cheer,
But such indulgence doth my health and sleep impair,
And I must hustle more, as if to reach the top,
Sacrificing discipline and rest, to climb the stair.

But oh, how I long for the carefree life of a farmer,
Where neighbours are like family, and the land doth call,

Where exercise and sleep are natural and bountiful,
And the city's hustle and bustle is but a distant thrall.

But alas, I am trapped in this concrete jungle,
Where the air is thick with pollution, and the noise never ends,
Where the people rush past, with no time for a smile or a jest,
Where my soul and my body both begin to unravel and unstrung.

But in the Ri-Bhoi valley, I can imagine the peace,
The sound of the river flowing, the birds singing in the trees,
The smell of freshly cut grass, the warmth of the sun on my face,
And the sense of belonging that I can never find in this place.

I dream of the day when I can leave this city behind,
And find my way to the valley, where my heart truly lies,
Where I can be free from the chaos and the stress,
And live my life as a farmer, beneath the clear blue skies.

But for now, I am trapped in this overcrowded and dirty city,
Yearning for the freedom and carefree life of a farmer in the Ri-Bhoi
valley,
Where neighbours and villagers are like families,
And where I can truly feel alive and healthy.

But even as I dream of this idyllic life,
I cannot help but feel a sense of guilt and shame,
For I have chosen this path as a lawyer,
And to leave it all behind, would be to play a different game.

For I have worked hard to achieve what I have,
And to leave it all behind, would be a waste,
But my heart aches for the simplicity of the village,
And the peacefulness that I cannot find in this place.

So I am torn between two worlds, and two lives,
The one I have chosen, and the one I long for,
And I cannot help but wonder, if I have made the right choice,
Or if I have lost sight of what truly matters, forevermore.

But perhaps one day, I will find a way to reconcile,
These two worlds, and these two lives,
And live the life of a lawyer, and a farmer,
In the overcrowded and dirty city, and the peaceful Ri-Bhoi valley.

But for now, I am stuck in this limbo,
Of wanting both, but unable to have it all,
And I am left to ponder on the paths I've taken,
And the choices that have led me to this bitter fall.

And as I walk the streets of this overcrowded city,
I cannot help but remember the calm of the valley,
And the simple pleasures that I once had,
And how they were replaced with misery and malady.

But perhaps, one day, I will find a way,
To leave this city and return to the valley,
Where I can live a life of simplicity,
And find the peace and happiness I've been craving.

Until then, I will continue to yearn,

For the freedom and carefree life of a farmer,

In the Ri-Bhoi valley, where I truly belong,

And where my heart and soul can finally be unfettered.

# 7. The Raven's Eternal Plight: A Dark Ode to Love and Fate

But the Raven's words, so dark and dreary, left my heart aching and sore
For they spoke of death and sorrow, of a love forever gone
And the finality of fate, that our lives are but a song

With a voice that echoed through the ages, the Raven spoke of Dante's plight
Of the journey through the circles, where the damned are doomed to fight
Of the souls trapped in the Inferno, and the ones who reach the skies
Of the eternal punishment and the eternal paradise

I longed to join the journey, to witness the eternal fate
To see if love endures, or if it's but a fleeting state
To see if the Raven's words were true, or if they were just a lie
But alas, I knew my fate, for I was doomed to die

So I stood there, staring at the Raven, with its eyes so dark and deep
And I knew that I had reached the end, and that my soul would soon to reap
For the Raven had spoken truth, and the truth was harsh and grim
And in that moment, I knew that my life was but a whim

But even as I faced my end, I couldn't help but wonder
If there was something more, if there was something asunder
For though the Raven's words were true, they left my heart in doubt
For if love endures, then what is life all about?

So I asked the Raven one last time, before my soul would flee
"Is there something more, is there something that I should see?"
And the Raven replied, in its voice so dark and low
"There is nothing more, for death is the end, and love is but a show."

# 8. Rustic Reverie: A Homage to Syadheh

In Syadheh, Ri Bhoi my childhood village, nestled at the base of Lum Sohpetbneng,

the rustic huts and sounds of animals formed a symphony of nostalgia.

The aroma of 'Ktung wait' our favourite dry fish cooked in 'Ka Lung Sei' our homemade bamboo shoot,

mingled with the pungent scent of 'U Niangryndia' , a delicacy of worm.

Cows and ponies ambled by as lullabies for the village's babes.

The presence of 'Thlong Dung Kba' , a traditional woody fence,

reminded us of our connection to the land.

We lived simply, using bamboo as glass and banana leaves as plates,

unfamiliar with the advancements of television,

but steeped in our own indigenous knowledge and techniques.

We ate from our backyard gardens, 'Khlaw Raid',

and caught fish from the river with traditional bamboo nets.

We embraced the heat of the sun as we worked our fields,

our soles as hard as steel from walking barefoot.

Nature was our mother, and we showed our gratitude through worship and respect.

We laughed at simple jokes and humors,

and fasted to test our discipline and resilience.

We walked miles daily, to the fields, to our homes, to the river.

We bathed with Sohpiengrah, nature's own soap.

In Syadheh, we lived in harmony with one another,

knowing only love and support.
A metaphor for life, in its purest, simplest form.


In Syadheh, we were one with the earth and all its creatures.
We knew the value of hard work and the satisfaction of a job well done.
The simplicity of our lives taught us to appreciate the small things,
the beauty in the mundane, the wonder in the natural world.
But as I stood there, revisiting my village of innocence and struggles,
I couldn't help but reflect on the changes that have occurred.
The modernization that has crept in, the loss of tradition,
the disconnection from the land and from each other.
But as I took in the sights and sounds and smells of my childhood,
I was reminded of the importance of preserving the past,
of holding onto the simplicity and purity of life.
For in Syadheh, I was reminded that it is in these moments,
these small, rustic villages, where we truly live.
Where we are truly alive.
Where we truly understand the meaning of life.
And so, I vow to carry this with me,
to hold onto the values of my village,
to always remember the simplicity and beauty of life in Syadheh.


As I walked through the streets of my village,
memories flooded back, each one a precious treasure.
I remembered the days spent playing with friends,
exploring the hills and rivers, and running through the fields.
I remembered the warmth of community, the sense of belonging.
In Syadheh, we were all connected,

each of us a vital piece in the tapestry of life.
We shared in each other's joys and sorrows,
and we worked together to make our village thrive.

But as I looked around, I saw that things had changed.
The village was not as I remembered it,
the traditions and customs that had once been so important
were now a thing of the past.
I realized that it was up to me, and others like me,
to preserve the memory of Syadheh,
to keep its spirit alive in the modern world.

So I made a vow to myself,
to do my part in keeping the legacy of Syadheh alive.
To share its stories and its traditions with others,
and to always remember the lessons it had taught me.
For in Syadheh, I had learned the true meaning of life,
the beauty of simplicity and the importance of community.
And those lessons would stay with me forever.

As I walked away from my village,
I knew that a part of me would always be there,
in the rustic huts and the rolling hills,
in the laughter and the tears,
in the memories of my childhood days.
Syadheh will always be a part of me,
and I will always be a part of Syadheh.

And so, I bid farewell to my village,

with a heart full of gratitude,

for the memories and the lessons it had given me.

I knew that I would return one day,

to reconnect with my roots and to remember the past,

to learn from the present and to look forward to the future.

Syadheh, my village of innocence and struggles,

the village where I truly understood the meaning of life.

And I will always be grateful for that.


As I walked away from Syadheh,

I felt a sense of longing and nostalgia.

I knew that I would never truly be able to leave my village behind.

It was ingrained in my being,

a part of me that would always be present.


I thought about how the world is constantly changing,

and how it is up to us to hold onto the things that matter.

For me, Syadheh represented simplicity, tradition,

and a deep connection to the natural world.

These were values that I knew were important,

and that I wanted to carry with me for the rest of my life.


I realized that in order to truly honor my village,

I needed to take action.

I needed to do my part in preserving its memory,

and in spreading its lessons to others.

I wanted to share the story of Syadheh,

to show others the beauty and wisdom that it held.

As I walked away, I knew that this would be my mission,
to keep the spirit of Syadheh alive.
I would work to educate people about the importance of tradition,
of simplicity, and of connection to the natural world.

I would do my best to make sure that the memory of Syadheh,
my village of innocence and struggles,
lived on, not just in my own heart,
but in the hearts of others, too.
For I knew that the lessons of Syadheh were universal,
and that they could benefit all who were willing to learn.
And I knew that in this way, Syadheh would always be with me,
and I would always be with Syadheh.

As I walked away from Syadheh,
I felt a sense of peace and contentment.
I knew that my village would always hold a special place in my heart,
and that I would always carry its lessons with me.

But as I looked to the future, I also knew that there was more work to
be done.
I knew that in order to truly honor Syadheh,
I needed to continue to learn and grow.
I needed to seek out new knowledge and new ways of understanding,
so that I could better share the story of my village with others.

I made a commitment to myself to continue to learn about the world,
to explore new cultures and new perspectives,
and to always be open to new ideas.

I knew that in order to truly honor Syadheh,
I needed to be a lifelong learner,
constantly seeking out new ways to understand and appreciate the world around me.

As I walked away from Syadheh,
I knew that my journey was just beginning.
But I also knew that with the lessons and values of my village in my heart,
I was ready to take on the world,
to share the story of Syadheh with others,
and to make a positive impact on the world in my own way.

Syadheh, my village of innocence and struggles,
will always be a part of me.
And I will always be a part of Syadheh.
And through my actions, the legacy of Syadheh will live on,
inspiring generations to come.

As I walked away from Syadheh,
I felt a sense of responsibility and purpose.
I knew that the lessons and values of my village,
were not just for me, but for the world.
I knew that in sharing the story of Syadheh,
I could inspire others to live a life of simplicity, tradition and connection to the natural world.

I knew that I had to be an advocate for the environment,
to educate people about the importance of sustainability and

conservation.
I knew that I had to spread the message of community and togetherness,
to promote the value of supporting each other and working together.

I knew that I had to be a voice for my village,
to ensure that its memory and legacy would be passed on to future generations.
I knew that I had to be a leader,
to inspire others to follow in my footsteps and to make a difference in the world.

As I walked away from Syadheh,
I knew that my journey had just begun.
But I was confident and determined,
knowing that with the lessons and values of my village in my heart,
I could make a real difference in the world.

Syadheh, my village of innocence and struggles,
will always be a part of me.
And I will always be a part of Syadheh.
And through my actions, the legacy of Syadheh will live on,
inspiring generations to come, to live a life of simplicity, tradition and connection to the natural world.

As I walked away from Syadheh,
I felt a sense of hope and optimism.
I knew that the lessons and values of my village,
could serve as a model for the world.

A world where people live in harmony with nature,
where tradition and culture are respected and preserved,
where community and togetherness are valued above all else.

I knew that I had a duty to use the knowledge I gained from my village,
to help others understand the importance of living a sustainable lifestyle.
To educate people about the importance of preserving the environment for future generations.
To promote the idea of living a simple life,
where material possessions are not the measure of success,
but where happiness and contentment are found in living in harmony with nature and community.

As I walked away from Syadheh,
I knew that my work was not yet done.
But I was determined to continue my journey,
to spread the message of my village far and wide,
to inspire others to learn from its lessons,
and to make a positive impact on the world.

Syadheh, my village of innocence and struggles,
will always be a part of me.
And I will always be a part of Syadheh.
And through my actions, the legacy of Syadheh will live on,
inspiring generations to come, to live in harmony with nature,
tradition, culture and community.
A world where we all can truly thrive.

As I walked away from Syadheh,
I felt a sense of purpose and responsibility.
I knew that the lessons and values of my village,
could be a guide for others.
A guide for a life where one can find balance,
between the natural and the man-made,
between tradition and modernity.

I knew that I had to use my experiences and knowledge,
to help others understand the importance of preserving traditional
ways of life.
To educate people about the importance of respecting and preserving
culture and heritage.
To promote the idea of living a balanced life,
where modernity and tradition can coexist,
where progress and preservation are not mutually exclusive.

As I walked away from Syadheh,
I knew that my journey was far from over.
But I was determined to continue my quest,
to spread the message of my village and its lessons,
to inspire others to learn from its wisdom,
and to make a positive impact on the world.

Syadheh, my village of innocence and struggles,
will always be a part of me.
And I will always be a part of Syadheh.
And through my actions, the legacy of Syadheh will live on,

inspiring generations to come, to strive for balance,
between nature, tradition, culture and modernity.
A world where we can live in harmony and find true fulfillment.


As I walked away from Syadheh,
I felt a sense of longing and sadness.
I knew that my village was a place of simplicity and purity,
a place where life was lived in harmony with nature.
But as I looked around, I could see that the world was changing,
and that the way of life in Syadheh was slowly disappearing.


I knew that I had to do my part to preserve the memory of my village,
to make sure that its lessons and values were not forgotten.
I knew that I had to be an advocate for the environment,
to educate people about the importance of sustainability and
conservation.
I knew that I had to spread the message of community and
togetherness,
to promote the value of supporting each other and working together.


As I walked away from Syadheh,
I knew that my journey was not yet complete.
But I was determined to continue my mission,
to share the story of my village with others,
to inspire others to learn from its wisdom,
and to make a positive impact on the world.


Syadheh, my village of innocence and struggles,
will always be a part of me.

And I will always be a part of Syadheh.
And through my actions, the legacy of Syadheh will live on,
inspiring generations to come to live a life of simplicity, tradition and
connection to the natural world.
A world where we can all truly thrive, in harmony with nature.

And I knew that I would continue this journey,
to keep the memory and legacy of Syadheh alive,
to inspire others to learn from its wisdom,
and to make a positive impact on the world.
For the sake of my village, for the sake of the future,
and for the sake of humanity.

# 9. The Burden of Secrecy

Verily, secrets kept in silence oft do weigh
Heavy upon the heart, a burden great,
For truth concealed doth fester and decay,
Eroding trust and fostering false estate.
But wisdom, e'er a treasure to be sought,
Should not be locked away, but freely shared,
For knowledge kept in secrecy is nought
But ignorance, a future unprepared.

The grave, a final resting place for all,
Should not be burdened with secrets kept,
For though in death the body may enthrall,
The mind and soul do onward still accept.
Let wisdom guide us in our mortal days,
And secrets be left to wither and to fade away.

But some may argue that secrets kept,
Are for the greater good, a necessary plight,
To protect oneself or those one has met,
From harm or malice, wrong or injustice right.

Yet wisdom tells us that in truth and light,
Lies the path to peace, and not in shadows deep,
For secrets held too tightly can ignite
A fire of mistrust, and love and friendship reap.

So let us strive to balance well the scales,
Between the need for secrecy and the call for truth,
For wisdom's voice should guide us, and not tales
Of fear or greed, in wisdom's light, our youth.

For in the end, when life's journey is through,
It is not secrets, but wisdom, that will see us through.

And as we journey through this mortal coil,
Let us not forget that wisdom's voice,
Is not confined to but a select few,
But echoes through the hearts of all, by choice.

For wisdom is not something to possess,
But something to be sought, and shared, and lived,
A guiding light, that brings us happiness,
And peace, and understanding, unachieved.

So let us all strive to seek wisdom's light,
And share it freely, as we go along,
For wisdom's path, is the path of right,
And secrets, best left, in the grave, belong.

For in the end, it's wisdom, not secrets, kept,
That shapes our legacy, and guides us to our final rest.

But let us not forget, that wisdom too
May come in different forms, and from diverse places,

It may be found in silence, or in words that are true,
In the simplest of actions, or the most profound faces.

Wisdom may come from our elders' sage advice,
Or from the innocent eyes of a child,
It may be found in the stars, or in the rolling dice,
In the beauty of nature, or in the struggles that pile.

So let us keep an open heart and mind,
To the wisdom that surrounds us all,
For it is in embracing it, we will find,
The answers to the secrets that call.

For wisdom is not a possession, but a journey,
That will guide us through life, and to our final return.

And as we journey on this path of wisdom,
Let us not forget the importance of balance,
For too much secrecy can lead to kingdom,
And too much wisdom, to confusion and chaos.

We must find the balance that works for us,
And make our choices with care and intention,
For wisdom is not a one-size-fits-all fuss,
But a journey that requires attention.

So let us not be afraid of secrets kept,
But let us also not let wisdom sleep,
For in the end, it is wisdom we'll have swept,

And secrets, in the grave, forever keep.

For wisdom is the light that guides us through,
The secrets are but shadows, fleeting and untrue.

As we navigate this mortal plane,
Let us remember that wisdom and secrets,
Are but two sides of the same coin, that contains
The choices we make, and the paths we select.

Wisdom tells us to be true to ourselves,
And to live with integrity and grace,
Secrets, on the other hand, remind us of the shelves,
That we build around us, to hide our face.

But as we journey through life's twists and turns,
Let us not forget that the ultimate goal,
Is to find harmony between wisdom and secrets, and learn
To use them both to make us whole.

For in the end, it is not secrets or wisdom alone,
But the balance between them, that will guide us home.

As we journey through this mortal life,
Let us remember that wisdom and secrets,
Are not mutually exclusive, but rather in strife,
To help us navigate the complexities.

For wisdom tells us to be honest and true,

To live with integrity and compassion,
Secrets, on the other hand, remind us to be shrewd,
And to protect ourselves from harm's imposition.

But as we make our choices and take our stands,
Let us not forget that the ultimate goal,
Is to find equilibrium between wisdom's commands,
And secrets' protective role.

For in the end, it is not secrets or wisdom alone,
But the balance between them, that will lead us to a peaceful home.

So let us strive to find that balance,
And to use wisdom and secrets, in harmony and balance.

As we journey through the sands of time,
Let us remember that wisdom and secrets,
Are not adversaries, but rather in a bind,
To help us navigate the complexities of life.

For wisdom tells us to be honest and true,
To live with integrity and empathy,
Secrets, on the other hand, remind us to be shrewd,
And to protect ourselves and those around us, discreetly.

But as we make our choices and take our stands,
Let us not forget that the ultimate goal,
Is to find the balance between wisdom's commands,
And secrets' protective role.

For in the end, it is not wisdom or secrets alone,
But the balance between them, that will lead us to a peaceful home.

So let us strive to find that balance,
And use wisdom and secrets, in harmony, for the betterment of all.

As we traverse the paths of life,
Let us remember that wisdom and secrets,
Are not adversaries, but rather in strife,
To help us navigate the complexities of existence.

For wisdom tells us to be honest and true,
To live with integrity and empathy,
Secrets, on the other hand, remind us to be shrewd,
And to protect ourselves and others, discreetly.

But as we make our choices and take our stands,
Let us not forget that the ultimate goal,
Is to find the balance between wisdom's commands,
And secrets' protective role.

For in the end, it is not wisdom or secrets alone,
But the balance between them, that will lead us to a peaceful home.

So let us strive to find that balance,
And use wisdom and secrets, in harmony, for the betterment of all.

For it is only in finding this balance,

That we can truly live a life, without regret or malice.

As we journey through the winding roads of fate,
Let us remember that wisdom and secrets,
Are not in opposition, but rather in harmony, to create
A well-rounded perspective on the complexities of life.

For wisdom tells us to be honest and true,
To live with integrity and empathy,
Secrets, on the other hand, remind us to be shrewd,
And to protect ourselves and others, discreetly.

But as we make our choices and take our stands,
Let us not forget that the ultimate goal,
Is to find the balance between wisdom's commands,
And secrets' protective role.

For in the end, it is not wisdom or secrets alone,
But the balance between them, that will lead us to a peaceful home.

So let us strive to find that balance,
And use wisdom and secrets, in harmony, for the betterment of all.

For it is only in finding this balance,
That we can truly live a life, with purpose and meaning, and without
regret or malice.

As we journey through the winding roads of fate,
Let us remember that wisdom and secrets,

Are not in opposition, but rather in harmony, to create
A well-rounded perspective on the complexities of life.

For wisdom tells us to be honest and true,
To live with integrity and empathy,
Secrets, on the other hand, remind us to be shrewd,
And to protect ourselves and others, discreetly.

But as we make our choices and take our stands,
Let us not forget that the ultimate goal,
Is to find the balance between wisdom's commands,
And secrets' protective role.

For in the end, it is not wisdom or secrets alone,
But the balance between them, that will lead us to a peaceful home.

So let us strive to find that balance,
And use wisdom and secrets, in harmony, for the betterment of all.

For it is only in finding this balance,
That we can truly live a life, with purpose and meaning, and without
regret or malice.

Let us remember that wisdom and secrets,
Are but tools on our journey, to be used with care,
For in the end, it is not the accumulation of them,
But the balance between them, that will lead us to a life fair.

As we traverse the winding roads of fate,

Let us remember that wisdom and secrets,
Are not in opposition, but rather in harmony, to create
A well-rounded perspective on the complexities of life.

• 53 •

For wisdom tells us to be honest and true,
To live with integrity and empathy,
Secrets, on the other hand, remind us to be discreet,
And to protect ourselves and others, judiciously.

But as we make our choices and take our stands,
Let us not forget that the ultimate goal,
Is to find the balance between wisdom's commands,
And secrets' protective role.

For in the end, it is not wisdom or secrets alone,
But the balance between them, that will lead us to a peaceful home.

So let us strive to find that balance,
And use wisdom and secrets, in harmony, for the betterment of all.

For it is only in finding this balance,
That we can truly live a life, with purpose and meaning, and without
regret or malice.

Let us remember that wisdom and secrets,
Are but tools on our journey, to be used with care,
For in the end, it is not the accumulation of them,
But the balance between them, that will lead us to a life fair.

So let us seek wisdom, and keep our secrets, with balance and grace,
For it is in this balance, that true wisdom, and true living, we will embrace.

• 54 •

# 10. The Enigma of Self

Verily, identity doth oft perplex the mind
A concept so elusive, yet so entwined
With every fiber of our being, it doth bind
A labyrinthine puzzle, for which none can find

The key to unlock the secrets of the self
A quest for which all souls do surely delve
Through the winding paths of life, we stealth
In search of that which makes us unique and wealth

But what is identity, truly, at its core?
Is it the sum of experiences we adore?
The culmination of the roles we have in store?
Or something deeper, that doth forever soar?

Perchance, identity is but a mere construct
A figment of the mind, a fleeting effect
A transient notion, that doth soon deflect
Leaving us to ponder, with nary a respect

Or mayhap, identity is a divine spark
A piece of the cosmic, that doth leave its mark
An essence that endures, through the trials dark
Guiding us towards truth, and the eternal arc

Identity doth remain
A mystery profound, without any certain gain
But in the quest for self, we shall sustain
And find our way, through the trials and the pain.

But as we journey on, and our souls unfurl
We may find that identity is a fluid swirl
Ever-changing, adapting to the world
A reflection of our growth, and the tales we've unfurled

For each experience shapes us in its way
Molding and shaping, with each passing day
And as we learn, and love, and live, we sway
Towards a truer version of ourselves, we'll weigh

Thus, identity is not a thing set in stone
But a dynamic force, that will forever roam
Through the annals of time, it will be shown
That we are not one, but many selves, unknown

So let us embrace the journey of the self
And all the identities that we may delve
For in the end, it is our unique wealth
And the key to understanding the universe itself.

In this ever-shifting kaleidoscope of life,
We can find a sense of self, free from all strife,
And let our true identity, free from all the strife
Shine like a beacon, through the endless night.

But in this quest for self, we must also beware
For identity can oft become a snare
A trap in which we lose ourselves, ensnared
In the illusions of the ego, we are ensnared

We must learn to let go of the self we knew
And embrace the unknown, in all its hues
For only in letting go, can we truly pursue
The true essence of identity, and what it imbues

For identity is not a fixed state to cling
But a fluid journey, on which we will wing
And as we fly, we'll discover new things
And find new selves, with each step we bring

So let us embrace the mystery of the self
And all the identities that we may delve
For in the end, it is our unique wealth
And the key to understanding ourselves.

In the end, identity is not a destination, but a journey
A path that we walk, with each step, we learn and discover,
And that journey is what makes life worth living and makes us unique,
For as we continue to explore, we continue to uncover.

As we traverse this winding road of life
We'll encounter many trials and strife
But through it all, our identity will thrive

For it is in the struggles that we truly come alive

For our identity is not just who we are
But also the choices we make, near and far
It is the sum of our actions, both good and mar
And the mark we leave, upon the world's scar

Thus, let us strive to be true to ourselves
And live with integrity, on the shelves
Of our being, let our actions speak for themselves
And let our identity shine, like a bright star,

But also be humble and open to change,
And the perspectives of others, let it arrange
Your understanding, and the self-knowledge that you gain
Will lead you to a more fulfilled life, and a more meaningful range

Identity is a complex thing
A tapestry woven, with threads of many a string
But in the journey to discover it, we'll find our wing
And soar to new heights, on the winds of self-discovery, we'll sing.

And as we continue on this journey of self-discovery,
We must remember to embrace the entirety,
Of who we are, the good and the bad,
For it is only through acceptance that we truly radiate.

For to suppress or ignore certain parts of ourselves
Is to do a disservice to the complexity of our identity,

And to deny ourselves the opportunity,
To grow and evolve into the best version of ourselves, with humility.

So let us embrace all aspects of our being,
And see the beauty in the complexity of our seeing,
For it is through understanding ourselves,
That we can truly understand the world, and start living.

Identity is not a destination, but a journey,
And as we continue on this journey, let us not hurry,
For the beauty of the journey is in the discovery,
And the person we become, in the end, is our true glory.

And as we walk this path of self-discovery,
Let us not forget the power of community,
For it is through the reflection of others,
That we can gain a deeper understanding of ourselves, and our identity.

For no man is an island, and we are all connected,
By the threads of humanity, and the love we've projected,
And as we gain a greater understanding of ourselves,
We also gain a greater understanding of the world, and how we've affected it.

So let us not walk this path alone,
But with open hearts and open minds, let us roam,
For as we gain a deeper understanding of ourselves,
We also gain a deeper understanding of the world, and our place in it.

Identity is not a destination, but a journey,
And as we continue on this journey, let us not worry,
For the beauty of the journey is in the discovery,
And the person we become, in the end, is our true glory.

# 11. Kwai's Perpetual Legacy

And so, kwai continues to be served,
A simple leaf, yet with a history so grand,
A bond between the rich and poor, a tradition true,
An offering to guests, to friends, and even strangers too.
In the matrilineal society of Meghalaya,
Its legacy lives on, its essence still in view.

For kwai is not just a leaf, it is a view,
A perspective on life, on equality, on trust,
A reminder of the bond between the rich and poor, a due,
That even in the bleakest moments, honor can be mustered.
And so it is chewed, in happiness and in sorrow,
A symbol of the state's eternal tomorrow.

For kwai raises blood circulation, it is believed,
And keeps one accompanied on lonely travels,
A blessing for the body, a comfort for the soul,
A symbol of the state's hospitality, its resolve.
In the matrilineal society of Meghalaya,
Kwai will always be served, its legacy forever whole.

And so, let us raise a leaf of kwai, and view,
Its history, its tradition, its essence so grand,
A symbol of equality, a bond between friends so true,
An offering to guests, to kin, to strangers, to all,

In the matrilineal society of Meghalaya,
Where kwai will always stand, a tradition so tall.

• 62 •

# 12. Eterna Splendor: A Sonnet of Enduring Love

Amidst the boundless panorama of chronology and cosmography,
In my thorax doth persist a magnificence resplendent,
E'er ineffably conjoined with my immutable essence,
A treasure I am indebted for, so just.

This affection, indescribable and immaculate,
A rarity beyond all terrestrial perception,
A liaison that shall perpetually persist,
And thrive, like a celestial body, diurnal and nocturnal.

Vocabulary fails to convey its authentic import,
An understated locution at most,
But nonetheless, my devotion for thee shall not diminish,
It shall abide, in my cardiac organ, a steadfast declaration.

Like cosmic particulate that composes a brilliant nebula,
Our affection is fabricated from elements of elegance,
A cosmic energy that shall everlastingly be.

So let this sonnet be a token, equitable,
Of the affection that eternally, shall be present.

And let it serve as a reminder, dear,
Of the passion that burns within my breast,

A flame that shall never falter, nor fear,
But blaze forever, in its quest for rest.

For in your eyes, I see the universe,
And in your touch, I feel the stars align,
With every beat of my love-worn heart,
I know that you are forever mine.

So let this sonnet be a testament,
To the love that we share, so pure and true,
A bond that will not be broken or bent,
But forever, in our hearts, renew.

For in this vast expanse of time and space,
Our love is the one true light that guides our way.

And though the years may pass, and time may race,
Our love shall remain, a steadfast grace.

Like the unchanging constellations in the sky,
Our love will shine, eternally bright.
It will endure, through every trial and sigh,
A beacon of hope, in the darkest of night.

So let this sonnet be a pledge, my love,
Of the devotion that I hold so dear,
For in this vast expanse of time and space,
Our love is the one thing that will always be here.

So let us hold on tight, and never let go,
For in this love, forever, our souls will glow.

And let us not be swayed by doubts or fears,
For our love is stronger than any mortal tears.

It is a force that defies all explanation,
A mystery that only our hearts can know,
And as long as we have each other's hand,
Our love will continue to grow and flow.

So let this sonnet be a celebration,
Of the love that we share, so rare and true,
For in this vast expanse of time and space,
Our love is the one thing that will always be new.

So let us cherish every moment, dear,
For our love is the one thing that will always be here.

And let us look to the future with hope,
For our love will weather any kind of weather.

We'll sail through the storms and calm the waves,
For in each other's arms, we'll find our shelter.

Let this sonnet be a promise, my love,
Of the devotion that will never fade,
For in this vast expanse of time and space,
Our love is the one thing that will never change.

Through the ups and downs of life, we'll stand,
For our love is the one thing that will always withstand.

So let us hold on tight, and never let go,
For in this love, forever, our hearts will glow.

And let us not be swayed by distance or time,
For our love will conquer all boundaries.

With every beat of our hearts, we'll find a way,
To keep our love alive, and shining brightly.

Let this sonnet be a reminder, my dear,
Of the passion that burns within our souls,
A fire that will never falter or fear,
But burn forever, and make us whole.

So let us hold on tight, and never let go,
For in this love, forever, we'll grow old.

And as the years pass, and time moves on,
Our love will remain, a beautiful song.

So let us cherish every moment, dear,
For our love is the one thing that will always be here.

# 13. Beyond Winning: A Quest for Destiny

Verily, I am a winner, victorious in the sperm race,
One billion plus contenders, all vying for first place.
For I am the one, the chosen, the elite,
The one who has emerged, the one to complete.

But what does it mean, to be a winner in this strife?
Is it simply to be the one who has won the life?
Or is there more to it, a deeper meaning to see,
A purpose to fulfill, a destiny to be.

For I am not just a winner, but a vessel of fate,
A being of purpose, a player in the game of life's debate.
My existence is not just chance, but a part of a grand design,
A piece of the puzzle, that fits into a cosmic line.

And so I must ponder, as I stand in my victory,
What is the reason, for my existence, my destiny.
For to be a winner, is not just to have won a race,
But to fulfill one's purpose, and to leave a lasting trace.

So let me not rest, on my laurels of success,
But strive ever forward, to fulfill my purpose and progress.
For to be a winner, is not just a title to claim,
But a journey of self-discovery, and a quest to become one's true aim.

And so I must journey, on this path of self-discovery,
With open mind and heart, and a willingness to unearth.
For there is more to me, than just my winning of this race,
There is a greater purpose, that I must embrace.

With each step I take, and each breath I inhale,
I am reminded of my purpose, and my role to unveil.
For I am not just a winner, but a part of a grand scheme,
A player in the game of life, with a role to redeem.

And so I must strive, to reach my full potential,
To become the best version of myself, so that I may be essential.
For to be a winner, is not just to have won a race,
But to live a life of purpose, and to leave a lasting trace.

So let me embrace, my victory with humility,
For it is not just about me, but about the greater community.
For I am a winner, but more than that I am a being,
With a purpose to fulfill, and a destiny to be.

And so I must journey, on this path of self-discovery,
With open mind and heart, and a willingness to unearth.
For there is more to me, than just my winning of this race,
There is a greater purpose, that I must embrace.

With each step I take, and each breath I inhale,
I am reminded of my purpose, and my role to unveil.
For I am not just a winner, but a part of a grand scheme,

A player in the game of life, with a role to redeem.

And so I must strive, to reach my full potential,
To become the best version of myself, so that I may be essential.
For to be a winner, is not just to have won a race,
But to live a life of purpose, and to leave a lasting trace.

So let me embrace, my victory with humility,
For it is not just about me, but about the greater community.
For I am a winner, but more than that I am a being,
With a purpose to fulfill, and a destiny to be.

So, I must continue on this path, with steadfast resolve,
For the journey of self-discovery, is one that I must evolve.
For, the victory of the sperm race, is not the end,
But the beginning of a journey, that shall never bend.

For, the true victory, is to fulfill one's purpose,
And to leave a legacy, that shall endure.
For, I am a winner, but more than that I am a being,
With a purpose to fulfill, and a destiny to be.

And so I must strive, to be more than just a winner,
But to be a force for good, and to leave a lasting sinner.
For the victory of the sperm race, is not the end,
But the beginning of a journey, that I must transcend.

For, the true victory, is not just to survive,
But to thrive and to flourish, and to come alive.

For, I am a winner, but more than that I am a being,
With a purpose to fulfill, and a destiny to be.

And so, I must embrace, my victory with grace,
And to use it as a stepping stone, to reach a higher place.
For, the victory of the sperm race, is not the end,
But the beginning of a journey, that I must transcend.

For, the true victory, is not just to have won,
But to be a true winner, and to live a life of fun.
For, I am a winner, but more than that I am a being,
With a purpose to fulfill, and a destiny to be.

So let me continue on this path, with courage and boldness,
For the journey of self-discovery, is one that I must harness.
For, I am a winner, but more than that I am a being,
With a purpose to fulfill, and a destiny to be.

And so I must strive, to reach for the stars,
And to push beyond my limits, and to push past my bars.
For, the victory of the sperm race, is not the end,
But the beginning of a journey, that I must transcend.

For, the true victory, is not just to have won,
But to be a true winner, and to live a life of fun.
For, I am a winner, but more than that I am a being,
With a purpose to fulfill, and a destiny to be.

And so, I must embrace, my victory with pride,
And to use it as a stepping stone, to reach the other side.
For, the victory of the sperm race, is not the end,
But the beginning of a journey, that I must transcend.

For, the true victory, is not just to have won,
But to be a true winner, and to live a life of fun.
For, I am a winner, but more than that I am a being,
With a purpose to fulfill, and a destiny to be.

So let me continue on this path, with hope and determination,
For the journey of self-discovery, is one that needs no hesitation.
For, I am a winner, but more than that I am a being,
With a purpose to fulfill, and a destiny to be.

# 14. Euphoric Enigma

Emotion, a force so powerful and profound,
A mystery that confounds, yet always surrounds.
A symphony of feelings, both light and dark,
A force that can ignite, or leave us stark.

But what is this emotion, that we all feel?
Is it simply a chemical reaction, or something more real?
Is it a product of our environment and upbringing,
Or is it an intrinsic part of our being?

Perhaps it is a combination of both,
A delicate dance between nature and growth.
For emotion is not just a simple thing,
But a complex and multifaceted being.

It can bring us to the heights of ecstasy,
Or plunge us into the depths of agony.
It can make us feel alive, or make us feel dead,
It can make us love, or make us hate, instead.

But without emotion, what would life be?
A monotone existence, with no depth or glee.
For emotion is what makes life worth living,
It gives us purpose and meaning, a reason for giving.

So let us embrace our emotions, with open hearts,
For they are a part of us, and will always play their part.
For emotion is not just a simple thing,
But the very essence of our being.

But with great power comes great responsibility,
For our emotions can lead us to both joy and adversity.
It is important to understand and control them,
To use them for good, and not let them overwhelm.

For when we let our emotions rule our actions,
We may regret the things we've said and done, in fractions.
But when we can master our emotions,
We can make wise decisions, and avoid commotions.

Emotion is a force that can shape our destiny,
It can lead us to greatness, or make us miserable.
But with self-awareness and mindfulness,
We can harness the power of emotion, with steadfastness.

So let us embrace the beauty and the beast,
That is emotion, and find inner peace.
For it is through our emotions, that we truly live,
And it is through our emotions, that we truly give.

Emotion is the very essence of our being,
It is what makes us human, and gives us meaning.
So let us embrace our emotions, with open hearts,
And find the balance between the light and the dark.

For emotion is not just a fleeting thing,
But a guiding force that shapes our journey's ring.
It can make us soar, or make us fall,
But through it all, it is the call.

Emotion is the fire that fuels our dreams,
It is the wind that carries our wings.
It is the light that guides us through the night,
And the warmth that keeps our souls alight.

But emotion can also be a curse,
If we let it control us, without any verse.
For too much of any emotion, can bring us to our knees,
And make us lose sight of what is truly meant to be.

So let us find the balance, in our hearts and minds,
And use our emotions, to make our lives more refined.
For emotion is not just a simple thing,
But a complex and powerful force, that shapes everything.

Let us embrace our emotions, with open hearts,
And find the beauty, in every part.
For emotion is the very essence of our being,
And it is through our emotions, that we truly find meaning.

Emotion is the thread that weaves our lives,
A tapestry of feelings, that never dies.
It is the passion that drives us to achieve,

And the love that makes us truly believe.

It is the laughter that brings us joy,
And the tears that give us a sense of poise.
For emotion is not just a transient thing,
But a force that shapes our destiny, like a ring.

But sometimes our emotions can be overwhelming,
And leave us feeling lost, and yearning.
It's important to take a step back and reflect,
To find the balance, and not neglect.

For when we can understand and control our emotions,
We can make better choices, and avoid commotions.
It's all about finding the equilibrium,
And not letting our emotions, become an obstacle.

Emotion is a powerful force, that gives us depth,
It's what makes life worth living, and gives us breadth.
Let us embrace our emotions with open hearts,
For they are the very essence of our being, and the art.

But we must also remember, that emotions are fleeting,
And they come and go, like the seasons beating.
We must learn to let them pass, like the tide,
And not let them control us, with too much pride.

For when we can detach ourselves from our emotions,
We can see things more clearly, with more devotion.

We can find inner peace and serenity,
And not let our emotions, control our destiny.

Emotion is a powerful force, that gives us life,
But it is important to find balance, to avoid strife.
For when we can master our emotions,
We can live a life of fulfillment and devotion.

So let us embrace our emotions, with open hearts,
And use them as a tool, to make our lives more smarts.
For emotion is not just a simple thing,
But a powerful force, that shapes everything.

Emotion is the very essence of our being,
It is what makes us human, and gives us meaning.
Let us embrace our emotions, with open hearts,
And find the beauty, in every part.

# 15. Illuminative Inquiry

So let us all take a moment to reflect,
On the beauty and power of light, correct,
For it's a force that's both elegant and grand,
And will continue to enlighten us, hand in hand.

And as we delve deeper into its secrets,
We find that light has many facets,
From the infrared to the ultraviolet,
Each wavelength with its own unique trait.

But light is not just a passive thing,
It also plays a role in everything,
From photosynthesis to the Northern Lights,
Light is a force that sets the world alight.

In the realm of cosmology,
Light helps us understand our history,
From the cosmic microwave background,
To the distant quasars that astound.

But with all its wonder and its might,
Light also brings the darkness of the night,
For when it's absorbed, it's no longer seen,
And that's the mystery of light that's yet to glean.

So let us all raise a glass to light,
A force that's both mysterious and bright,
For it's the very essence of our being,
And the key to understanding everything.

And as we delve into the future,
We see the potential for light to nurture,
In fields like medicine and communication,
Light holds the key to innovation.

From the development of optical fibers,
To the use of light in cancer therapies,
The possibilities are endless and exciting,
With light as the guiding light in our quest for enlightenment.

But with all the benefits that light brings,
We must remember to use it with care and think,
For too much light pollution can obscure the stars,
And lead to negative effects on life on Mars.

So let us all strive to use light responsibly,
And to appreciate its beauty and its diversity,
For light is a force that enriches our lives,
And helps us navigate through time and space with ease.

It's a force that's both mysterious and grand,
Guiding us through the vastness of the land,
It's the essence of our being and the key to understanding everything,
Light, the force that brings us all together, shining.

And as we look to the future,
We see the potential for light to capture
The secrets of the universe and unlock new realms,
With cutting-edge technology at the helm.

From the study of gravitational waves,
To the search for exoplanets and their ways,
Light holds the key to uncovering the unknown,
And expanding our understanding of the cosmos grown.

But light also holds the potential to create,
In fields like art, design and architecture,
Where the manipulation of light can evoke emotion,
And shape our perceptions of the world in motion.

So let us all marvel at the wonder of light,
And its ability to both reveal and ignite,
For it's a force that's both mysterious and grand,
Guiding us through the vastness of the land.

And as we continue to explore and discover,
Let us never forget the power of light's cover,
For it's the very essence of our existence,
A force that illuminates and guides us to persistence.

And as we journey through the ages,
We come to realize the many stages,
That light has undergone in its evolution,

From the dawn of time to the present revolution.

From the Big Bang's cosmic radiation,
To the formation of galaxies in motion,
Light has played a vital role in shaping,
The universe we know, and its mapping.

And as we look to the future,
We see the potential for light to capture,
The secrets of the universe and unlock new realms,
With cutting-edge technology at the helm.

But light is not just a force in the cosmos,
It also plays a crucial role in our daily doses,
From the way we see and communicate,
To the way we heal and innovate.

So let us all appreciate the gift of light,
And its ability to both reveal and ignite,
For it's a force that's both mysterious and grand,
Guiding us through the vastness of the land.

And as we delve deeper into the mysteries of light,
We come to realize the true complexity of its might,
From the quantum mechanics of its wave-particle duality,
To the ways in which it interacts with reality.

From the phenomena of interference and diffraction,
To the mysteries of quantum entanglement and action,

Light continues to confound and astound us,
As we strive to unlock its secrets and trust.

But light also holds the power to inspire,
With its beauty and radiance that can never tire,
From the aurora borealis to the rainbow's hue,
Light is a force that captivates and renews.

So let us all marvel at the wonder of light,
And its ability to both reveal and ignite,
For it's a force that's both mysterious and grand,
Guiding us through the vastness of the land.

And as we continue to explore and discover,
Let us never forget the power of light's cover,
For it's the very essence of our existence,
A force that illuminates and guides us to persistence.

And as we ponder on the mysteries of light,
We realize the importance of its role in the fight,
Against the darkness that threatens to engulf us,
Light stands as a beacon of hope and trust.

From the stars that guide us through the night,
To the fire that warms us and brings delight,
Light has been a constant companion throughout history,
Helping us navigate through life's mystery.

But light also holds the power to create,

In fields like art and photography,
Where the manipulation of light can evoke emotion,
And shape our perceptions of the world in motion.

So let us all appreciate the gift of light,
And its ability to both reveal and ignite,
For it's a force that's both mysterious and grand,
Guiding us through the vastness of the land.

And as we continue to explore and discover,
Let us never forget the power of light's cover,
For it's the very essence of our existence,
A force that illuminates and guides us to persistence.

And as we about to come to the end of our epic journey,
We realize the true significance of light's story,
It's a force that has shaped our world in countless ways,
And will continue to do so in the future days.

From the beginning of time to the present age,
Light has been a constant on life's stage,
It's a force that weaves its way through all of life,
Guiding us through the joys and the strife.

But light also holds the power to transcend,
To bring about a sense of unity and blend,
As we come together under its radiance,
We are reminded of our shared existence.

So let us all appreciate the gift of light,
And its ability to both reveal and ignite,
For it's a force that's both mysterious and grand,
Guiding us through the vastness of the land.

And as we continue to explore and discover,
Let us never forget the power of light's cover,
For it's the very essence of our existence,
A force that illuminates and guides us to persistence.

And as we look to the future,
We see the potential for light to nurture,
In fields like quantum computing and cryptography,
Light holds the key to solving the world's complexity.

From the use of light-based qubits to process information,
To the use of light-based encryption to protect communication,
The potential for light to shape our technological advancements,
Is truly an exciting and promising enhancement.

But light also holds the power to unite,
In the face of global challenges and fight,
As we come together under its radiance,
We are reminded of our shared existence and resilience.

So let us all appreciate the gift of light,
And its ability to both reveal and ignite,
For it's a force that's both mysterious and grand,
Guiding us through the vastness of the land.

And as we continue to explore and discover,
Let us never forget the power of light's cover,
For it's the very essence of our existence,
A force that illuminates and guides us to persistence.

And as we come to the end of our epic,
We realize the true significance of light's topic,
It's a force that has touched every aspect of our lives,
And will continue to do so as our knowledge derives.

From the smallest particles to the grandest galaxy,
Light has been a constant in the cosmic tapestry,
It's a force that holds the key to understanding,
The mysteries of the universe, and its expanding.

But light also holds the power to connect,
Bringing us together and respecting,
The diversity and beauty of our world,
Under its radiance, we are all unfurled.

So let us all appreciate the gift of light,
And its ability to both reveal and ignite,
For it's a force that's both mysterious and grand,
Guiding us through the vastness of the land.

And as we continue to explore and discover,
Let us never forget the power of light's cover,
For it's the very essence of our existence,

A force that illuminates and guides us to persistence.

# 16. A Morsel of Mortality

Oh food, the sustenance of life, the fuel for our being,
A source of pleasure and nourishment, a constant redeeming
But what is it that makes food so much more than mere sustenance?
Is it the taste, the texture, the memories it evokes with persistence?

Perhaps it is the way it brings people together, a bonding force,
Sharing a meal with loved ones, a social intercourse
Or maybe it is the way it reflects our culture and our past,
A reflection of our heritage, a history that will forever last.

But as we partake in this feast, let us not forget the plight
Of those who go hungry, with no food in sight
For as we indulge in excess, there are those who lack
Let us not forget our responsibility, to share and give back.

So let us savor each bite, with gratitude and grace,
For the gift of food, a blessing in this earthly place.
And let us strive to ensure, that all may share in this treasure,
For food is not just sustenance, it is a fundamental pleasure.

And yet, as we delve deeper into the thoughts of food,
We must also consider the ethical implications, not to be viewed
As mere sustenance, but as a moral quandary,
For the choices we make in what we eat, have a profound impact on
our society.

From factory farming to deforestation, the cost of our sustenance
Is one that is paid by the earth, and all its inhabitants
And so we must ask ourselves, what is the true cost of our repast?
And strive to make choices that will truly make our future last.

For food is not just about nourishing our bodies, but our souls as well,
It has the power to connect us to one another, and to a higher dwell
But it also has the power to harm, if we do not tread with care,
Let us remember, that with great power, comes great responsibility to
bear.

So let us ponder the deep mysteries of food,
As we partake in this feast, let us be in a contemplative mood
For food is not just sustenance, but a philosophical conundrum,
That has the power to shape our lives, and the world in which we
succumb.

As we delve deeper into our thoughts of food,
we must also consider the impact on our mood.
Food has the power to alter our emotions,
to bring us pleasure, or to cause commotions.

Certain foods have been known to boost our mood,
while others have been linked to depression and brood.
It is important to be mindful of what we consume,
and to strive for a balance, rather than to assume.

Food is not just about nourishment, but also about pleasure,

But let us not forget, that too much of a good thing, can lead to leisure.
Moderation is key, in all that we eat,
For a balanced diet, is the foundation of a healthy treat.

In conclusion, food is not just sustenance, but a complex affair,
It is a source of pleasure, culture, and ethical care.
Let us strive to make conscious choices, in all that we eat,
For food is not just sustenance, but a fundamental treat.

As we continue to delve deeper into the philosophy of food,
we must also consider the impact on our attitude.
Food has the power to shape our perspectives,
to make us see the world in different spectacles.

The way we approach food, can impact our overall well-being
It can be a source of stress or it can be a source of healing.
It is important to have a positive relationship with food,
to see it as a source of nourishment, and not as something crude.

Food is not just about sustenance, it is also about connection,
It is a reminder that we are all human, and have a shared affection.
It has the power to bring people together, to break down barriers
And to remind us that we are all part of a larger picture.

In conclusion, food is not just sustenance, it is a multi-faceted entity
It is a source of pleasure, culture, ethics, and serendipity.
Let us strive to make conscious choices, in all that we eat,
For food is not just sustenance, it is a fundamental treat that is complete.

# 17. The Divine Dilemma

In public discourse, the topic of God
Is oft a source of heated debate and strife,
With some who claim belief in deity,
And others who reject such notion as life.

But what is it that makes us question thus
The very existence of a higher power?
Is it the lack of evidence, or trust
In man's own intellect and reason's tower?

Perchance, it is a fear of something great,
That lies beyond our mortal understanding,
And thus, we cling to our own self-made fate,
Refusing to accept what fate is demanding.

But let us not forget that faith is blind,
And in the end, true truth we may not find.

Perhaps, in public discourse we should seek
To understand, and not to simply speak.
For surely, in our human frailty,
We cannot comprehend infinity.

So let us not in arrogance presume
To know the mind of God, who's thoughts are pure.

But let us humbly seek, and listen, assume
That there may be a greater allure.


For in this world of chaos, pain, and strife,
The thought of God brings hope, and gives new life.


And so, in public discourse, let us strive
To seek the truth, and not just take and give.
For in the end, the truth will always thrive,
And in its light, our souls will truly live.


So let us not be swayed by pride or fear,
But seek the truth, and in it, let us hear.


For in this search for truth, we must not fear
To question, doubt and challenge all we know,
For in this quest, we may find what is dear,
And in this quest, our minds and hearts may grow.


For in this quest, we may come to realize
That what we thought we knew, was but a guise,
And in this quest, we may come to surmise
That God is not a being, but a flow.


A flow of love, a flow of grace and peace,
A flow that moves through all of time and space,
A flow that guides us to eternal bliss,
And in this flow, we find our resting place.

So let us not in public discourse fight,
But seek the truth, and in it, find the light.

For in this search for truth, we must not hide,
Our doubts and fears, but let them be exposed,
For in this quest, we may find what is right,
And in this quest, our souls may be composed.

For in this quest, we may come to accept,
That God is not a being, but a force,
A force that shapes the world, that we can't detect,
But in its presence, we can sense its source.

A force that gives us strength, when we are weak,
A force that guides us, when we feel lost,
A force that brings us hope, when we are meek,
And in this force, we find our hearts embossed.

So let us not in public discourse hate,
But seek the truth, and in it, find our fate.

For in this search for truth, we must not shy,
Away from questions, that may seem absurd,
For in this quest, we may find the why,
And in this quest, our souls may be unburied.

For in this quest, we may come to realize,
That God is not a being, but a mystery,
A mystery that may never be surmised,

But in its wonder, we find our destiny.

A mystery that gives us purpose, and drive,
A mystery that shapes our every breath,
A mystery that keeps us alive,
And in this mystery, we find our death.

So let us not in public discourse mock,
But seek the truth, and in it, find our lock.

For in this search for truth, we must not falter,
In the face of opposition and dissent,
For in this quest, we may find what we alter,
And in this quest, our souls may find contentment.

For in this quest, we may come to embrace,
The idea that God is not a thing,
But a concept, that we cannot trace,
But in its essence, we feel its ring.

A concept that gives us meaning, and hope,
A concept that shapes our every thought,
A concept that helps us to cope,
And in this concept, we find what we sought.

So let us not in public discourse divide,
But seek the truth, and in it, find our guide.

For in this search for truth, we must not yield,

To the temptations of ignorance and pride,
For in this quest, we may find what is revealed,
And in this quest, our souls may be sanctified.

For in this quest, we may come to see,
That God is not a thing, but a presence,
A presence that surrounds us constantly,
And in its aura, we find our essence.

A presence that gives us love and light,
A presence that guides us through the dark,
A presence that brings us to the right,
And in this presence, we find our mark.

So let us not in public discourse separate,
But seek the truth, and in it, find our fate.

For in this search for truth, we must not falter,
In the face of doubt and disbelief,
For in this quest, we may find what we alter,
And in this quest, our souls may find relief.

For in this quest, we may come to understand,
That God is not a thing, but a concept,
A concept that is both grand and grand,
And in its grandeur, our souls are excepted.

A concept that brings us peace and joy,
A concept that shapes our every step,

A concept that brings us to the employ,
And in this concept, we find our rep.

So let us not in public discourse divide,
But seek the truth, and in it, find our guide.

For in this search for truth, we must not fear,
To question, doubt and challenge all we know,
For in this quest, we may find what is dear,
And in this quest, our minds and hearts may grow.

For in this quest, we may come to realize,
That God is not a being, but a mystery,
A mystery that may never be surmised,
But in its wonder, we find our destiny.

A mystery that gives us purpose, and drive,
A mystery that shapes our every breath,
A mystery that keeps us alive,
And in this mystery, we find our death.

So let us not in public discourse mock,
But seek the truth, and in it, find our lock.

For in this search for truth, we must not falter,
And in the quest, we find our own altar.

For in this search for truth, we must not yield,
To the temptations of simplicity,

For in this quest, we may find what is concealed,
And in this quest, our souls may find humility.

For in this quest, we may come to see,
That God is not a thing, but a concept,
A concept that is both complex and free,
And in its complexity, we are exempt.

A concept that brings us wisdom and growth,
A concept that shapes our every thought,
A concept that helps us to know,
And in this concept, we find what we sought.

So let us not in public discourse divide,
But seek the truth, and in it, find our guide.

For in this search for truth, we must not falter,
And in the quest, we find our own altar.

For in this search for truth, we must not shy,
Away from the unknown and the unseen,
For in this quest, we may find what is high,
And in this quest, our souls may find serene.

For in this quest, we may come to understand,
That God is not a thing, but a presence,
A presence that is both near and grand,
And in its grandeur, our souls find recompense.

A presence that brings us guidance and light,
A presence that shapes our every step,
A presence that helps us to do what is right,
And in this presence, we find our rep.

So let us not in public discourse divide,
But seek the truth, and in it, find our guide.

For in this search for truth, we must not falter,
And in the quest, we find our own altar.

For in this search for truth, we must not stop,
To seek the answers that elude our minds,
For in this quest, we may find what is on top,
And in this quest, our souls may find new binds.

For in this quest, we may come to realize,
That God is not a thing, but a mystery,
A mystery that may never be surmised,
But in its wonder, we find our destiny.

A mystery that gives us hope and light,
A mystery that guides us through the dark,
A mystery that brings us to the right,
And in this mystery, we find our mark.

So let us not in public discourse mock,
But seek the truth, and in it, find our lock.

For in this search for truth, we must not falter,
And in the quest, we find our own altar.

# 18. The Noble Navigator

Leadership, a virtue oft debated and sought,
A trait that doth inspire and guide the masses,
A beacon in the night, a light unsought,
A path to greatness, free from dire impasses.

But what doth make a leader truly great?
Is it the strength of will, the force of might?
Or doth it lie in wisdom, to debate
And guide with reason, leading to the right?

Perchance, the true mark of a leader's worth
Is found in deeds, not words alone. A girth
Of action, bold and unafraid, to birth
Progress, to guide the ship that's tossed and torn.

Thus, leadership is not a state bestowed
But earned through deeds, a path to be trod.

And so, in this pursuit of leadership true,
We must strive to be more than what we're viewed.
We must be selfless, putting others first,
And in our actions, show integrity and trust.

For true leadership is not about command,
But rather, serving with a selfless hand.

It's not about the power we possess,
But the good we bring, the lives we touch and bless.

So let us strive to be the leaders we admire,
With hearts of gold and souls that truly fire,
For in this world of chaos and despair,
We need more leaders who truly care.

And as we lead, let us not forget
The fragility of life and our own debt
To those who came before and pave the way,
And those who will come after us to stay.

For leadership is not a solitary quest,
But a journey shared by all who care to invest
In making this world a better place,
With a strong and steady hand to guide the race.

So let us be the leaders that we need,
With courage, strength, and wisdom as our creed,
For in this world of turmoil and unrest,
We need true leaders who will do their best.

And as we lead, let us not be blind
To the struggles that others face unkind
For true leadership is not just for the strong
It's for those who can empathize and belong.

Let us be the leaders that bridge divides,

And break down barriers that keep us confined
For leadership is not about control
But about bringing people together as a whole.

Let us be the leaders who show the way
And inspire others to rise and to sway
For true leadership is not about fame
It's about making a difference in this game.

In this quest for leadership that we undertake
Let us strive to be the best versions of our own fate.

And as we lead, let us not forget
The role of humility, to be met
With open hearts and open minds, to learn
From those around us, and not to yearn

For power or prestige, but to be true
To ourselves and those we serve, to do
What's right, and to make a lasting impact
In the lives of those we lead, to act

With integrity, compassion, and grace
To be the best leaders we can be, to face
The challenges ahead with strength and poise
And to leave a legacy that will not be noise

For true leadership is not about the fame
But about making a difference and leaving a name.

And as we lead, let us not forget
That leadership is not a one-time set
It's a constant evolution and growth,
To adapt and improve, to learn and both

Lead and be led, to humble ourselves
And admit to mistakes, to find the wealth
Of wisdom in the diverse perspectives,
To lead with empathy, and to connect

With those we serve, to build a strong foundation
Of trust and respect, to lead with compassion
For true leadership is not just a role
But a journey, with a heart and a soul

So let us be the leaders that we ought
To be, with courage and wisdom, that's bought
By the experiences of life, and the will
To make a difference, to lead and to thrill.

And as we lead, let us not forget
The importance of being self-reflect
To constantly evaluate and improve
Our own actions, and to always move

Towards progress, towards a greater good
For ourselves and for all those we should
Lead and serve, to be the best versions

Of ourselves, to lead with fair intentions

And to make a lasting impact on the world
To leave behind a legacy unfurled
Of leadership that was truly great,
That inspired and uplifted, to create

A better future for all those we lead
With honor, integrity, and with speed
For true leadership is not just a feat
But a journey, with a noble end to meet.

And as we lead, let us not forget
That true leadership is not a one-man bet
It's a team effort, a collective goal
To achieve success, and to roll

With the punches, to lead and to follow
To work together and to hallow
The spirit of collaboration and trust
To lead with integrity, and to thrust

Forward towards progress, and to leave
A lasting impact, to achieve
The greater good, for all and not just a few
For true leadership is not a pursuit

Of power or prestige, but a quest
To make a difference, to be the best

We can be, and to lead with honor
For all those we serve, and to foster

A better future, for all.

And as we lead, let us not forget
That true leadership is not a one-time set
It's a lifelong journey, a daily grind
To always strive to be one step ahead of the mind

To constantly evolve, adapt and improve
To stay relevant, and to always move
Towards progress and the greater good
For all those we lead, and for the hood

Of humanity, to lead with purpose
To make a lasting impact, and to disperse
Wisdom, guidance, and inspiration
To all those who seek, for the sensation

Of true leadership is not just a role
But a way of life, with a heart and a goal
To make a difference, to lead and to thrive
And to leave a legacy, that will always survive.

And as we lead, let us not forget
That true leadership is not a power to get
But a responsibility to uphold
And to use for the betterment of old

And young, to lead with empathy and care
To understand, and to be aware
Of the struggles of those we lead
And to be a constant source of seed

Of hope, to lead with integrity and grace
And to be a guiding light in this race
For progress, to lead with humility
And to be open to learning, so we can see

The bigger picture and make the right call
For true leadership is not about standing tall
But about making a difference for all.

And as we lead, let us not forget
That true leadership is not a conquest,
But a journey of self-discovery,
To understand ourselves and our own query.

To lead, we must first understand
Our own strengths, weaknesses and command
To know our own purpose and goal
And to strive towards a common role.

True leadership is not a title or crown
But a state of mind, to wear it with renown
And humility, to lead with compassion
And to leave a lasting impression.

For true leadership is not about fame
But about making a difference, to claim
A legacy, that will be remembered
For the good it brought, and for being tendered.

So let us lead with honor and pride
For the betterment of all, side by side.

And as we lead, let us not forget
That true leadership is not a one-time bet
But a continuous process, to evolve
And to improve, to involve

All those we lead, to foster a sense
Of community, to build up a fence
Of trust and respect, to lead with fairness
And to always be aware of the rareness

Of this opportunity, to make a change
To lead with purpose and to not estrange
Ourselves from the struggles of those we lead
For true leadership is not about being ahead

But about being in it together, to strive
For a better future, to keep alive
The spirit of progress and to leave
A lasting legacy, that will be perceived

As true leadership, a beacon of hope,
A shining example, to help us cope
In this journey of life.

And as we lead, let us not forget
That true leadership is not a one-man act
But a collaboration, to work as one
With a common goal, and not to shun

The ideas and perspectives of others
For true leadership is not just for brothers
But for all, regardless of race, gender, or class
For true leadership is not about the brass

But about making a difference, to leave
A lasting impact, to achieve
The greater good, for all and not just a few
For true leadership is not a pursuit

Of power or prestige, but a quest
To make a difference, to do our best
And to lead with honor and integrity,
For all those we serve, and to be

A shining example, a role model,
A true leader, with a heart and a soul,
For all to follow and be inspired.

And as we lead, let us not forget

That true leadership is not a one-way street
But a two-way dialogue, to listen
And to hear the voices of those glisten

With ideas and perspectives, to lead
With empathy, and to take heed
Of the needs of those we serve, to strive
For a better future, to keep alive

The spirit of progress and to leave
A lasting legacy, that will be perceived
As true leadership, a beacon of hope,
A shining example, to help us cope

In this journey of life, to lead with grace
And to make a difference, to leave a trace
Of positive change, for all to see
That true leadership is not just a destiny

But a choice, a responsibility,
A journey to be taken, with humility.

And as we lead, let us not forget
That true leadership is not a one-dimensional set
But a multidimensional, holistic approach
To lead with integrity, and to encroach

On the various aspects of life, to lead
With empathy, and to take heed

Of the needs of those we serve, to strive
For a better future, to keep alive

The spirit of progress and to leave
A lasting legacy, that will be perceived
As true leadership, a beacon of hope,
A shining example, to help us cope

In this journey of life, to lead with grace
And to make a difference, to leave a trace
Of positive change, for all to see
That true leadership is not just a destiny

But a choice, a responsibility,
A journey to be taken, with humility.

And as we lead, let us not forget
That true leadership is not a one-time debt
But a lifelong commitment, to learn
And to grow, to take our turn

To guide and inspire, to lead with grace
And to make a difference, to leave a trace
Of positive change, for all to see
That true leadership is not just a destiny

But a journey, a continuous process
Of self-discovery, to access
The best version of ourselves, to lead

With integrity, and to take heed

Of the needs of those we serve, to strive
For a better future, to keep alive
The spirit of progress and to leave
A lasting legacy, that will be perceived

As true leadership, a shining example
Of a leader who made a difference, ample.

# 19. The Fickle Pursuit of Vitality

Verily, health doth elude the grasp of many,
A fickle mistress, oft allusive and wan.
An enigma wrapped in mystery, a chancy
Pursuit, for which the wisest man doth plan.

Forsooth, in health doth lie the key to life,
The very essence of our earthly stay.
Without it, all the wealth and fame and strife
Are but a fleeting dream, a transient day.

But what is health, and how doth it abide?
Is it a state, a virtue, or a goal?
Perchance, 'tis but a fleeting thing, a tide
That ebbs and flows, and waxes, wanes, and rolls.

Some say that health is but a balance kept
Betwixt the body, mind, and spirit true.
A harmony of being, where hath crept
No sickness, pain, nor any malady new.

Others argue that health is but a quest
A journey to be taken day by day.
A striving for perfection, at its best
A never-ending path to find one's way.

Perchance, the truth doth lie in both, my friend
For health doth balance being, and doth blend
The body, mind, and spirit to ascend
To a higher state, in which to comprehend
The beauty and the wonder of it all
And in this journey, to stand tall.

Forsooth, in health, doth lie the key to life,
The very essence of our earthly stay.
Without it, all the wealth and fame and strife
Are but a fleeting dream, a transient day.

Therefore, let us cherish health above
All else, for it is the elixir of love
That doth sustain us, and doth fill our cup
With joy, with peace, with beauty, and with hope.

But alas, not all are blessed with good health,
For some are burdened with disease and pain.
Their bodies wracked with torment, their wealth
Of days consumed by suffering and strain.

Yet even in the darkest hour, there glows
A spark of hope, a beacon shining bright.
For health, though fickle, doth come and goes
But the human spirit doth endure the fight.

For health is not just mere physical state

But also a mental and emotional quest
To find a balance, to transcend our fate
And rise above the trials that distress.


And so, let us not take our health for granted
But strive to nurture and preserve it well
For in its absence, all is supplanted
By sorrow, grief, and a living hell.


Let us embrace the journey of good health
With open hearts and minds, and strive for wealth
Of days filled with vitality and strength
And let our spirits soar to immeasurable length.


For in the end, it is not length of days
But the richness of life, that truly pays.
The true measure of success is health
For in it, lies true happiness and wealth.


But, alas, the pursuit of health is not
Without its trials and tribulations.
For oft, the path to wellness is fraught
With obstacles, both physical and mental.


Society's ills, the toxic environment,
The pressures of the modern world, all play
Their part in hindering our quest for health,
And making the journey harder day by day.

We must, however, not be disheartened,
For though the road may be long and winding,
We must remember that we are not defeated,
And that there is always hope in finding.

We must strive to break the shackles that bind,
The ones that keep us from our true selves.
We must seek out healthier ways of living,
And strive to improve our mental and physical health.

For in the end, it is our own actions
That shape our lives, and determine our fates.
So let us take control, with full conviction,
And pave the way towards healthier states.

Let us remember
That health is not a destination, but a journey,
A constant pursuit, an endeavor
Towards a better, more fulfilling future.

So let us strive for health, with all our might
For in it, lies the key to leading a life that is truly bright.

But, as we strive for health, let us not forget
The importance of empathy and care
For those who suffer, and who are beset
With illness and affliction, everywhere.

For health is not just a personal quest,

But a collective responsibility.
We must strive to build a society that is just,
And ensure that all have access to health care.

We must work to break the barriers of class,
And end the systemic discrimination
That keeps so many from achieving health,
And traps them in a cycle of deprivation.

We must also be mindful of our impact
On the environment, and strive to preserve
The planet that sustains us, and to act
To mitigate the harm that we observe.

For true health is not just about the self,
But also about the greater good.
It is about creating a world that is fair,
And in which all can live, and thrive, and should.

So let us strive for health, not just for ourselves,
But for all of humanity, and the earth,
Let us work towards a brighter future,
And build a world of health, peace, and worth.

But let us not forget the role of fate
In shaping the course of our health journey.
For though we strive and make our choices great,
There are some things that are beyond our control, and blurry

We must learn to accept the cards we're dealt
And make the most of every single day.
For in the end, it is our inner self
That will guide us through the twists and turns along the way.

For health is not just a destination
But a journey, with its ups and downs,
A balance between effort and elation
And learning to appreciate the present not just the crowns.

So let us strive for health, with humility
And grace, in all we do and say.
For in the end, it is not wealth or fame
But health, that truly leads to a life fulfilled each day.

In conclusion, let us embrace the quest
For health, with courage, and with zest,
For in the end, it is the ultimate test
Of our character, and our worth as human, it is the best.

# 20. The Cost of Liberty: An Exploration of Individual Autonomy and Community Interdependence

With liberty as our inalienable right,
We oft' forget the weight that freedom bears.
For though we're free to choose our own true fight,
The choices made can lead to endless cares.

Do we, in fact, possess true autonomy?
Or are our actions but predetermined?
Are we but pawns in some grand game of fate,
Or masters of our own existence?

Perchance, true freedom lies within the mind,
Where thoughts and dreams are free to take their flight.
And though the world may seek to bind and bind,
The human spirit shall forever fight.

For freedom's not a gift, but hard-earned prize,
Won through the trials of life's bitter ties.

But is this freedom worth its lofty cost,
This constant struggle for the right to be?

For in our quest for autonomy lost,
We oft' forget the beauty of community.

Perhaps true freedom lies in finding balance,
In striking harmony between the self and all.
Where every choice we make holds consequence,
But also holds the potential to enthrall.

And as we navigate this mortal sphere,
Let us not forget the ties that bind us all.
For in our quest for personal freedom dear,
We must not let our fellow man's rights fall.

For true freedom lies in empathy,
And love for all humanity.

But what of those who seek to take away,
This freedom that we hold so dear to heart?
Do we give in to their tyrannical sway,
Or do we stand and make a brand new start?

For freedom's not a thing that can be won,
Or taken by the strong and powerful.
It's a constant battle, to be fought and done,
By all who seek to make a change in the world.

So let us all strive for true autonomy,
With empathy and love as our guiding stars.
And let us all work towards true freedom,

For all mankind, near and far.

For freedom is not just for the few,
But for all, in all that we do.

And as we journey through life's winding roads,
Let us remember freedom's greater goal:
To live our lives as truest selves, unshackled by the loads
That others seek to place upon our soul.

For freedom is not license to do as we please,
But the right to be who we were meant to be.
And in this quest, may we find true release,
From all the chains that bind and limit thee.

So let us all embrace our liberty,
And strive towards a brighter destiny,
Where all may live in true autonomy,
And true freedom reigns eternally.

For in the end, it is not chains that bind,
But the mind's own limitations we must find.

And as we strive to break free from these binds
Let us remember, freedom's not an end,
But a journey of self-discovery,
A path that each must tread and comprehend.

For true freedom is not found in power or wealth,

But in the choices we make, the paths we tread,
In the love we give, the ties we create and the bonds we build,
And the way we live our lives, until the end.

Let us not take for granted this precious gift,
But cherish and nurture it every day.
For true freedom is a state of mind, a lift,
That takes us to the heights, where we can truly say

We are free. And in that freedom we find,
The truest form of human-kind.

But with this freedom comes great responsibility,
For with choice comes power, and with power comes change.
We must use our freedom wisely, with humility,
To make a better world, for ourselves and for all range.

For freedom is not just for our own gain,
But for the good of all, for the greater cause.
We must use our liberty to ease the pain,
And uplift the downtrodden, to right the wrongs.

And as we journey on, let us not forget,
The sacrifices made, the struggles fought,
To win this freedom, that we hold so dear,
And let us pass it on, to the next and the next, a legacy brought.

For freedom is not a destination,
But a journey, with no end or cessation.

In every step we take, in every breath,
We must strive to uphold this freedom's worth,
For it is not a prize to be possessed,
But a fire that burns within each hearth.

And though the road to freedom may be long,
And oft' beset with trials and with strife,
We must not falter in our quest,
For freedom is the essence of our life.

For in our freedom, we find the key,
To unlock the doors of hope and of dreams,
To reach for the stars, to soar and to be,
To live a life that truly gleams.

So let us cherish this freedom dear,
And make it a guiding light throughout the years.

# 21. Election fever grips the land : A Sestina to assembly election in India

Election fever grips the land, a fervor to unite,
A season of celebration, three months before the fight.
We dance and party like our lives are at their peak,
Forgetting all else, save for Gandhi's face on each note we seek.
Crazy for our candidate, we campaign day and night,
Fighting for their victory, ideology out of sight.

We stand for them, believing they'll bring prosperity,
But after the election, our hopes turn to adversity.
Our chosen candidate, now a stranger in our eyes,
Regrets creeping in, as we realize our foolish lies.

We thought we knew them, but they were mere facade,
Their true selves hidden, a political charade.

In ancient Rome and Greece, tales of betrayal abound,
Of leaders who promised much, but let their people down.
Like Caesar, who won the hearts of Rome with his charm,
But ultimately led to the Republic's downfall and harm.
Or Agamemnon, whose thirst for glory led to war,
Leaving his people in a state of despair evermore.

But perhaps, in the end, we are the true fools to blame,
For putting our trust in candidates who play the game.
Next time, let us be wiser, and truly see,
The true face of those who seek to lead and govern thee.

So let us join together, and in this election fervor,
Learn from our mistakes, and make a better future.

But as the election nears, the fever grips once more,
Our memories fade, and we're caught in its lure.
We dance and party, convinced that this time will be different,
That our candidate will bring us the change we're convinced is
imperative.

But as the votes are counted, and the results are clear,
We're left with a bitter taste, and a sense of fear.
For once again, our candidate has let us down,
Promising one thing and delivering another, a familiar frown.

We're left in a state of despair, wondering where we went wrong,
As we're left to pick up the pieces, and sing a different song.

But perhaps, in the end, it's not the candidate who's to blame,
But rather, our own blindness, and our desire for fame.
For in this never-ending cycle, we're the ones who choose,
And it's up to us to break the pattern, and make a better muse.

So let us come together, and in this election fever,
Learn from our mistakes, and make a brighter future.

For it's not just about the candidate, but about the change we seek,
And it's up to us to make it happen, and our future to reshape.

# 22. The Legacy of Likai: A Cautionary Fable in Cherrapunji

As the fable doth narrate, a damsel of solitary parentage,

By name Likai, didst reside in the hamlet of Rangjyrteh,

Upstream of the cataracts. She, being a sumpter,

Didst earn her livelihood by transporting iron

From Rangjyrteh to Mawmluh village. Ka Likai, labored long hours,

Oft away from home, leaving her infant progeny

In the charge of others. Subsequently, she didst enter into matrimony

A second time. However, her spouse didst bear ill-will

Towards the babe, and thus, the situation didst take a dire turn.

Upon her return from a day of toil, Likai didst find her offspring missing.

But, being greatly famished, she didst partake of the cooked flesh.

Thereafter, as she didst sit to slice betel leaves, as was the custom of the village,

She didst behold a tiny digit, which she didst recognize.

Realizing the horror of her actions, Likai was seized with grief and rage,

Which didst drive her to the brink of the cataract,

From whence she didst hurl herself into the abyss.

Noh in Khasi doth signify "jump." And thus, the cataract doth now bear the name

Noh-ka-Likai falls. Situated in Sohra as know by local people or by the world as Cherrapunji in Meghalaya,

The falls doth serve as a reminder of Likai's tragic fate,

A cautionary tale of the dangers of ill-will and rash actions.

But even in death, Likai's spirit doth live on,

Eternally etched in the name of the cataract,

A symbol of strength and resilience for all who reside

In the hamlet of Rangjyrteh and beyond. And though Likai labored long hours,

Oft away from home, her legacy doth remain,

A testament to the power of the human spirit,

And the importance of compassion and empathy, even in dire turn.

# 23. Euphoric Whispers: A Journey to Inner Peace

In joy's embrace, we oft perceive true bliss,
A state of mind where cares and woes are missed.
Yet is this happiness of fleeting stay,
A transient guest that comes and goes away.

Perchance true joy is but an ephemeral,
A mere illusion of the mortal sphere.
For though we chase it, still it doth evade,
And leaves us with a sense of emptiness.

Perhaps true happiness doth lie within,
In contemplation, and self-reflection.
Wherein we find true solace, and begin
To see the world with equanimity and affection.

Thus, let us not in vain pursuits engage,
But find true happiness in wisdom's sage.

And though the path to wisdom may be long,
With twists and turns that oft confound and wrong,
Yet in this journey, we shall find the strength,
To weather life's tumultuous lengths and breadth.

For wisdom brings a peace that passeth all,

A serenity that cannot be enthralled,
By fate's capriciousness, or luck's deceit,
For it is rooted deep in inner heat.

So let us strive to find true happiness,
In wisdom's light, and not in worldly excess,
For in the end, it is the wise man's bliss,
That truly stands the test of time's distress.

So let us seek the truth, and not despair,
For in the quest for wisdom, lies true happiness.

And as we traverse this path of life with care,
Let us not falter, nor in doubts immerse,
For happiness is but a state of mind,
And wisdom is the key that unlocks its door.

It is in learning, growing, and evolving,
That we find true contentment, and resolving
The struggles and the doubts that life may bring,
And see the beauty in the simplest thing.

So let us strive to find true happiness,
In wisdom's light, and not in worldly excess,
For in the end, it is the wise man's bliss,
That truly stands the test of time's distress.

So let us seek the truth, and not despair,
For in the quest for wisdom, lies true happiness.

And in this quest, we shall find peace, and air,
To breathe and live, and love, in true success.

But let us not forget that wisdom too,
Is not a destination, but a journey,
A constant quest for knowledge and the truth,
That leads us to a state of pure serenity.

For wisdom is the balance of the mind,
Between the heart and reason's logic kind,
It is the harmony of thought and feeling,
That brings a sense of purpose to our being.

So let us strive to find true happiness,
In wisdom's light, and not in worldly excess,
For in the end, it is the wise man's bliss,
That truly stands the test of time's distress.

So let us seek the truth, and not despair,
For in the quest for wisdom, lies true happiness.
And in this quest, we shall find meaning, where
We can live a life of purpose and completeness.

And in this quest, let us not be alone,
For wisdom shared is wisdom multiplied,
And joys and sorrows shared, are not our own,
But shared with friends and loved ones, they are lightened.

So let us seek the company of those,

Who share our quest for wisdom and true joy,
For in each other's company, we'll compose
A symphony of life, a cosmic ploy.

So let us strive to find true happiness,
In wisdom's light, and not in worldly excess,
For in the end, it is the wise man's bliss,
That truly stands the test of time's distress.

So let us seek the truth, and not despair,
For in the quest for wisdom, lies true happiness.
And in this quest, let us build a world, where
Love and empathy, the foundation, is.

For true happiness is not a solitary pursuit,
But one that thrives in the company of others,
It is in giving and receiving, in sharing and caring,
That we truly find the meaning of life and its wonders.

So let us strive to find true happiness,
In wisdom's light, and not in worldly excess,
For in the end, it is the wise man's bliss,
That truly stands the test of time's distress.

So let us seek the truth, and not despair,
For in the quest for wisdom, lies true happiness.
And in this quest, let us be kind and fair,
As we build a world, of love, and peace, and blessedness.

For true happiness is not a destination,
But a journey, that is best shared with others, on this foundation.

And as we journey on, let us not forget
The beauty of the world around us,
For nature's splendor is a true testament
To the wonder and the majesty of life.

Let us take time to pause and to reflect,
On all the gifts that life has to offer,
For in this gratitude, we'll truly connect
With the present, and our hearts will prosper.

So let us strive to find true happiness,
In wisdom's light, and not in worldly excess,
For in the end, it is the wise man's bliss,
That truly stands the test of time's distress.

So let us seek the truth, and not despair,
For in the quest for wisdom, lies true happiness.
And in this quest, let us embrace the air,
Of gratitude, and live in true completeness.

And let us not forget the power of hope,
For it is the beacon that guides us through,
The darkest of days, and helps us to cope
With life's difficulties, and all that's new.

For hope is the light that shines in the night,

And gives us the strength to carry on,
It is the wings that help us take flight,
And reach new heights, beyond the dawn.

So let us strive to find true happiness,
In wisdom's light, and not in worldly excess,
For in the end, it is the wise man's bliss,
That truly stands the test of time's distress.

So let us seek the truth, and not despair,
For in the quest for wisdom, lies true happiness.
And in this quest, let us hold on to hope,
For it is the key that unlocks the door to true completeness.

And let us not forget the power of love,
For it is the binding force that holds us all,
It is the light that shines from above,
And guides us through life's rise and fall.

For love is the force that brings us together,
And gives us the strength to carry on,
It is the warmth that makes life worth living,
And the beacon that guides us home.

So let us strive to find true happiness,
In wisdom's light, and not in worldly excess,
For in the end, it is the wise man's bliss,
That truly stands the test of time's distress.

So let us seek the truth, and not despair,
For in the quest for wisdom, lies true happiness.
And in this quest, let us open our hearts to love,
For it is the key that unlocks the door to true completeness and peace.

And let us not forget the power of service,
For it is the act of giving back,
It is the way we make the universe
A better place, with every step we take.

For service is the way we make a difference,
And bring about positive change,
It is the way we transcend our existence,
And make a lasting impact, on the range.

So let us strive to find true happiness,
In wisdom's light, and not in worldly excess,
For in the end, it is the wise man's bliss,
That truly stands the test of time's distress.

So let us seek the truth, and not despair,
For in the quest for wisdom, lies true happiness.
And in this quest, let us serve with care,
For it is the key that unlocks the door to true completeness and peace.

And as we journey on this quest for wisdom,
Let us remember that true happiness
Is not a destination, but a state of being,
A state of mind, that comes with true understanding.

For wisdom is the key that unlocks the door
To true happiness and inner peace,
It is the light that guides us evermore,
And gives our lives a sense of purpose and release.

So let us strive to find true happiness,
In wisdom's light, and not in worldly excess,
For in the end, it is the wise man's bliss,
That truly stands the test of time's distress.

So let us seek the truth, and not despair,
For in the quest for wisdom, lies true happiness.
And in this quest, let us be true to ourselves,
And let our hearts and minds be at ease.

And as we journey on this quest for wisdom,
Let us remember to be kind and compassionate,
For the world needs more love and kindness
To heal the wounds and mend the brokenness.

So let us strive to find true happiness,
In wisdom's light, and not in worldly excess,
For in the end, it is the wise man's bliss,
That truly stands the test of time's distress.

So let us seek the truth, and not despair,
For in the quest for wisdom, lies true happiness.
And in this quest, let us be a source of hope,

And let our actions inspire others to seek the same.

For true happiness is not a solitary pursuit,
But one that we can share and spread, and that is the ultimate pursuit.

And as we seek true happiness and wisdom,
Let us not forget to be present in the moment,
To savor life's small joys and treasures,
And to appreciate the beauty of the world around us.

For the present is the only time we have,
And it is where true happiness is found,
In the simple things, and in the moments we savor,
And not in the pursuit of wealth or fame that surrounds.

So let us strive to find true happiness,
In wisdom's light, and not in worldly excess,
For in the end, it is the wise man's bliss,
That truly stands the test of time's distress.

So let us seek the truth, and not despair,
For in the quest for wisdom, lies true happiness.
And in this quest, let us live in the present,
And find joy in the journey, not just the destination.

And as we journey on this quest for wisdom,
Let us not forget to be self-compassionate,
For we are all human, and we are all imperfect,
And we all make mistakes, it's part of our nature.

Self-compassion is the key to self-acceptance,
And it is the key to true inner peace,
It is the way to overcome our self-doubts and hesitance,
And to be kind and gentle with ourselves, without cease.

So let us strive to find true happiness,
In wisdom's light, and not in worldly excess,
For in the end, it is the wise man's bliss,
That truly stands the test of time's distress.

So let us seek the truth, and not despair,
For in the quest for wisdom, lies true happiness.
And in this quest, let us practice self-compassion,
And learn to accept and love ourselves, as we are.

And as we journey on this quest for wisdom,
Let us not forget to practice forgiveness,
For it is the key that sets us free,
From the chains of the past, and its bitterness.

Forgiveness is the way to move on,
And to let go of the pain and the anger,
It is the way to heal the wounds,
And to find peace and inner strength, like no other.

So let us strive to find true happiness,
In wisdom's light, and not in worldly excess,
For in the end, it is the wise man's bliss,

That truly stands the test of time's distress.

So let us seek the truth, and not despair,
For in the quest for wisdom, lies true happiness.
And in this quest, let us practice forgiveness,
And learn to let go, and to move forward with life.

And as we journey on this quest for wisdom,
Let us not forget to be grateful,
For every breath we take, every step we make,
Is a blessing, a gift, a reason to be thankful.

Gratitude is the way to appreciate,
All the good things in life, big or small,
It is the way to find joy in the present,
And to live life to the fullest, standing tall.

So let us strive to find true happiness,
In wisdom's light, and not in worldly excess,
For in the end, it is the wise man's bliss,
That truly stands the test of time's distress.

So let us seek the truth, and not despair,
For in the quest for wisdom, lies true happiness.
And in this quest, let us practice gratitude,
And learn to be thankful for all that life has to offer.

And as we journey on this quest for wisdom,
Let us not forget to be humble and kind,

For in humility, we gain true wisdom,
And in kindness, we leave a positive footprint behind.

Humility is the way to understand,
That we are not always right, and that we can learn,
It is the way to respect others and to expand,
Our horizons, and our understanding to discern.

Kindness is the way to show compassion,
And to make a positive impact on others,
It is the way to spread love and affection,
And to make the world a better place for brothers.

So let us strive to find true happiness,
In wisdom's light, and not in worldly excess,
For in the end, it is the wise man's bliss,
That truly stands the test of time's distress.

So let us seek the truth, and not despair,
For in the quest for wisdom, lies true happiness.
And in this quest, let us be humble and kind,
And make a difference in the world, with our mind.

And as we journey on this quest for wisdom,
Let us not forget to be resilient and strong,
For life will throw obstacles in our way,
But it is up to us to rise above and carry on.

Resilience is the ability to bounce back,

From adversity, and to keep moving forward,
It is the way to find the strength to attack,
The problems, and to not let them be a hinder.

Strength is the way to face the challenges,
And to overcome them with courage and grace,
It is the way to find the inner balance,
And to not let the difficulties take the place.

So let us strive to find true happiness,
In wisdom's light, and not in worldly excess,
For in the end, it is the wise man's bliss,
That truly stands the test of time's distress.

So let us seek the truth, and not despair,
For in the quest for wisdom, lies true happiness.
And in this quest, let us be resilient and strong,
And face the challenges with courage, all along.

And as we journey on this quest for wisdom,
Let us not forget to be open-minded and curious,
For an open mind is a receptive mind,
And curiosity is the spark that ignites the fire within us.

Open-mindedness is the way to explore new ideas and perspectives,
And to broaden our understanding of the world,
It is the way to challenge our own beliefs and to be receptive
To the thoughts and opinions of others, so we can learn and unfurl.

Curiosity is the drive to seek knowledge,
And to discover new things, it is the fuel that keeps us going,
It is the way to challenge our own limits, and to acknowledge
That there is still so much to learn, and so much to be knowing.

So let us strive to find true happiness,
In wisdom's light, and not in worldly excess,
For in the end, it is the wise man's bliss,
That truly stands the test of time's distress.

So let us seek the truth, and not despair,
For in the quest for wisdom, lies true happiness.
And in this quest, let us be open-minded and curious,
And embrace the opportunity to learn, grow, and flourish.

And as we journey on this quest for wisdom,
Let us not forget to be patient and persistent,
For patience is the key to perseverance,
And persistence is the key to achieving success.

Patience is the ability to wait for the right moment,
To not rush into things, and to take our time,
It is the way to be mindful and present,
And to find peace in the journey, not just the climb.

Persistence is the ability to keep going,
To not give up, and to never lose sight,
It is the way to keep pushing through the obstacles,
And to achieve our goals, with all our might.

So let us strive to find true happiness,
In wisdom's light, and not in worldly excess,
For in the end, it is the wise man's bliss,
That truly stands the test of time's distress.

So let us seek the truth, and not despair,
For in the quest for wisdom, lies true happiness.
And in this quest, let us be patient and persistent,
And achieve our goals, with persistence.

And as we journey on this quest for wisdom,
Let us not forget to be self-aware and reflective,
For self-awareness is the key to understanding ourselves,
And reflection is the key to understanding our actions and their effects.

Self-awareness is the ability to understand our thoughts, feelings, and actions,
And to be aware of our strengths and weaknesses, it helps us to be true to ourselves and to our values.

Reflection is the ability to take a step back, and to analyze our actions and their consequences, it helps us to learn from our mistakes and to improve ourselves.

So let us strive to find true happiness,
In wisdom's light, and not in worldly excess,
For in the end, it is the wise man's bliss,
That truly stands the test of time's distress.

So let us seek the truth, and not despair,
For in the quest for wisdom, lies true happiness.
And in this quest, let us be self-aware and reflective,
And strive to understand ourselves and our actions, and constantly
improve ourselves to reach true completeness.

And as we journey on this quest for wisdom,
Let us not forget the importance of balance,
For balance is the key to a harmonious life,
And it is the key to finding true happiness.

Balance is the ability to find equilibrium,
Between different aspects of our lives,
It is the way to find harmony,
Between work and play, and between our internal and external strife.

So let us strive to find true happiness,
In wisdom's light, and not in worldly excess,
For in the end, it is the wise man's bliss,
That truly stands the test of time's distress.

So let us seek the truth, and not despair,
For in the quest for wisdom, lies true happiness.
And in this quest, let us strive for balance,
And learn to find harmony within ourselves, and in the world around
us.

And as we journey on this quest for wisdom,

Let us not forget the importance of self-improvement,
For self-improvement is the key to self-actualization,
And it is the key to reaching our full potential.

Self-improvement is the process of developing oneself,
Both personally and professionally, it is a lifelong journey that requires
dedication and persistence.

It is the way to gain knowledge, skills, and experiences,
And to become the best version of oneself.

So let us strive to find true happiness,
In wisdom's light, and not in worldly excess,
For in the end, it is the wise man's bliss,
That truly stands the test of time's distress.

So let us seek the truth, and not despair,
For in the quest for wisdom, lies true happiness.
And in this quest, let us strive for self-improvement,
And work towards becoming the best version of ourselves, and
reaching our full potential.

# 24. The Eloquent Odyssey: A Voyage of Introspection

Through winding paths of cerebral exploration,
We tread the realm of thoughts and contemplation.
With lexicon both rich and vast in scope,
We delve into the depths of introspection.

Our minds, a labyrinth of endless thought,
A place of musings, questions, and discourse,
With every step, a new concept is caught,
And language, our tool to guide us, of course.

But as we delve deeper, deeper still,
We find that words alone cannot suffice,
For thoughts that truly challenge and thrill,
Demand a lexicon both deep and precise.

So let us dive into the mind's abyss,
And with our words, unlock the secrets missed.

But with each new discovery we make,
We must remember, there's still so much at stake.
For every answer found, a hundred more,
Remain, waiting to be unlocked and explored.

Our quest for knowledge, a never-ending climb,

A journey that tests both body and mind.
And as we strive to understand our place,
We must remind ourselves to stay humble and grace.

For though our words may soar to great heights,
Our understanding, still so limited,
But with each new thought and insight,
We inch closer to truth, unbounded.

So let us continue on this quest,
To explore and understand our own mind,
For in this journey, we'll find the best,
And the true beauty, of being human kind.

But as we journey on, let us not forget,
The impact of our thoughts on those around,
For every action, every word we've said,
Has ripples that extend far and profound.

Let us use our language with care and heed,
For it shapes not just our own reality,
But also the world in which we all need,
To coexist in peace and harmony.

So let us use our words to lift and inspire,
To promote love and understanding,
For in this world of chaos and mire,
We must be a beacon of hope, standing.

And as we journey on, let us remember,
The power of our thoughts, our words, and our endeavor.

As we explore the depths of our mind,
Let us not forget that we are all entwined,
In a web of connections, both seen and unseen,
Each thought and action, affecting the whole, it seems.

Our journey of self-discovery,
Is not just for our own betterment,
But for the betterment of all humanity,
And the world in which we are all content.

So let us strive to understand ourselves,
But also to understand others and their wealth,
Of thoughts, feelings, and experiences,
For in empathy, true wisdom and understanding resides.

In this quest for knowledge and self-discovery,
Let us not forget to foster unity.

But as we navigate the winding paths,
Of our thoughts and introspection,
Let us not forget to take a step back,
And appreciate the beauty of the connection.

For though our minds may wander,
And our thoughts may race,
It is in the stillness we find the wonder,

Of being alive in this world, in this place.

Let us not get lost in the search,
For answers and understanding,
But let us find beauty in the process,
And cherish the mystery and wonderland.

So let us explore our thoughts with care,
And cherish the journey, as much as the air.

As we delve into the unknown,
And uncover the secrets of our mind,
Let us not forget to be shown,
That we are all connected and intertwined.

For in this vast and ever-expanding universe,
We are but a small and fleeting part,
But in our thoughts and our words, we immerse,
Ourselves in meaning and purpose.

Let us not be afraid to question,
To challenge and to seek,
For in the pursuit of truth and understanding,
We find ourselves and our place in the world, unique.

So let us continue on this journey,
With open minds and hearts,
For in the exploration of our thoughts,
We find ourselves, and where we truly belong to starts.

And as we explore the vast expanse,
Of our thoughts and introspection,
Let us remember to take a chance,
On new perspectives and new direction.

For though we may be comfortable in our own beliefs,
It is in the challenge of them that we grow,
And find new meaning and new reliefs,
In the perspectives we learn to know.

So let us not be afraid to question,
To challenge and to seek,
For in the pursuit of truth and understanding,
We find ourselves and our place in the world, unique.

Let us embrace the journey,
With open minds and hearts,
For in the exploration of our thoughts,
We find ourselves, and where we truly belong to starts.

As we continue on this journey of self-discovery,
Let us not forget to take time to reflect,
On the things we've learned, the things we've seen,
And how they've affected us, and our perspectives.

For in reflection, we can gain a new perspective,
On the things we thought we knew,
And in doing so, we can better connect,

With the world and the people around us, too.

So let us not be afraid to step back,
And take a moment to look within,
For in doing so, we can gain a new tack,
And a deeper understanding of our own skin.

In this journey of self-exploration,
Let us remember the value of reflection.

As we explore the depths of our mind,
And discover the secrets it holds,
Let us not forget to be kind,
To ourselves and our own souls.

For in this journey, we may stumble,
We may falter and we may fall,
But it is in the overcoming, we humble,
And rise stronger, standing tall.

So let us not be too hard on ourselves,
For the mistakes we make along the way,
For they are the stepping stones to wisdom and wealth,
And the means to a better tomorrow, today.

Let us embrace the journey,
With compassion and self-love,
For in the exploration of our thoughts,
We find ourselves and the power thereof.

As we continue to explore our thoughts,
Let us not forget the power of connection.
For in connecting with others, we're taught,
That we're not alone in our introspection.

By sharing our thoughts and our feelings,
We find understanding and support,
And in that, a sense of healing,
That helps us to press on and exhort.

So let us not be afraid to reach out,
And share our innermost thoughts,
For in doing so, we can help to dispel any doubt,
And find comfort in the company of those we're brought.

Let us continue on this journey of self-discovery,
With open hearts, open minds and connection, which is key.

As we explore the depths of our mind,
Let us not forget the beauty of simplicity.
For in the midst of complexity and confusion, we'll find
That sometimes, the simplest answers are the most profound, humility.

Let us not get lost in the intricacies of thought,
And forget to appreciate the present moment,
For it is in the quietude, we're taught,
The wisdom of mindfulness and contentment.

So let us strive for balance in our exploration,
Of the workings of our mind,
For in the harmony of simplicity and complexity,
We'll find true understanding, one that is kind.

In this journey of self-discovery,
Let us not forget to seek balance and simplicity.

# 25. The Leaf of Equality: A Sestina on Kwai

In the matrilineal society of Meghalaya,
A tradition holds strong and true,
Where kwai, a humble offering, is served,
To guests and friends, to kin and strangers too.
An important necessity in every household,
Its history rooted in a tale so grand.

A rich man and a poor, two friends did stand,
In a bond forged by their humble view,
That wealth and status hold no sway in society,
And in this bond, their friendship did ensue.
But sorrow struck, the poor had naught to serve,
His honor lost, he took his life with due.

The rich man, seeing the sacrifice so true,
Followed his friend in a final stand,
And the Gods, moved by their devotion,
Blessed the state with kwai, a simple offering.
The poorest now could offer something grand,
Their honor kept, their respect still due.

And thus, kwai became a symbol of equality,
Bridging the rich and poor, a simple bond,
Served in celebrations, served in funeral,

An act of friendship, an offering to the old.
And chewing kwai, it is believed, will serve,
As a blessing for the body, for the soul too.

In every household, kwai holds its due,
A tradition passed down, a tale so grand,
A symbol of equality, a bond so true,
The offering of friendship, to the young and old.
In the matrilineal society of Meghalaya,
Kwai will always stand, a tradition so true.

# 26. Transcendence in the Abyss of Despair

In every quaff we partake, with each libation,
We're confronted with the acrid truths of ephemerality,
That every evanescent pleasure, a mere sensation,
Is but an illusion, in this realm of causality.

For in this mortal sphere, where agony and tribulation predominate,
Our quest for significance appears futile,
And all our endeavors but lead to bitter lamentation,
A never-ending cycle of despondency, sans reprieve.

So let us elevate our goblets aloft in salute,
To all the sorrows, the afflictions we endure,
For in this cosmos of vacuity and coast,
The only verity is our despair.

But let us not relinquish hope, for in this despair,
Lies the potential for transcendence, for growth,
For in the face of our mortality, we can repair
Our understanding of life, and all that it entails, both.

Thus let us drink, and let us raise our chalice,
To all the sorrows, the tribulations we endure,
For in this existence of nothingness and mass,
The ultimate truth is our potential for maturation.

For in the depths of our despair, we find
The strength to rise above our mortal plight,
To transcend the fleetingness of time,
And find purpose in the struggle and the fight.

Let us not be swayed by transient joys,
For they are but illusions in the end,
But instead, let us embrace life's poise,
And strive to make our existence transcend.

For in this mortal realm, where pain and strife prevail,
There is still beauty to be found in all,
And in our struggles, we can surely unveil
The meaning that we seek, and stand tall.

So let us raise our goblets high in toast,
To the journey of life, and what it holds,
For in this mortal realm, there is much to boast,
And in our despair, much to behold.

# 27. The Pelican's Omen: A Sonnet on the Futility of Existence

Upon the ominous horizon, a pelican doth appear,

A portent of impending malaise, a harbinger of fear,

A symbol of the void that lies within the human heart,

The abyss that plagues us all, our acrimonious fate, a stark chart.


The mandible that gaped, the orbs that seemed to convey,

"Your aspirations and ideals, nought but a fleeting mirage",

Remind us of the futility of our mortal way,

The interminable cycle of life's onerous burden, a savage scourge.


The pelican, with its cavernous, yawning gullet,

Is but a reflection of our own desolation,

A manifestation of the emptiness we discerned,

In every facet of this unjust world, a bitter sensation.


We toil and contend, but to what end?

The pelican's yawn reminds us: oblivion awaits us in the end.

A cycle of birth and death, a never-ending spiral,

A Sisyphean task, our existence, a mere denial.


Thus, we must strive to transcend our mortal plight,

To find solace in the eternal, not in temporal might,

For in the end, it is the soul that truly matters,
Not the fleeting glories of this world, that are but tatters.

And so, we must embrace the pelican's ominous warning,
And strive to find meaning in our time here, fleeting and forming,
For in the face of our own mortality, we must not despair,
But seek to understand the purpose of our being, and repair

The emptiness we feel, the void within our hearts,
By seeking truth, love, and wisdom, and by taking part
In the grand scheme of things, by making our mark
On this world, in our own unique way, with love and spark.

For in the end, it is not the pelican's yawn that defines us,
But the actions we take, and the love we leave behind us.
So let us not be swayed by melancholy's song
But strive to live our lives with purpose and valor, all along.

And as we journey through this mortal coil,
Let us not forget the pelican's toil,
For in its yawn, we see our own reflection,
A reminder of our own mortality's direction.

But let us not be overcome by despair,
For in this life, there is still much to repair,
Let us strive to leave a lasting legacy,
And in the end, true immortality to see.

For in this world, there is much beauty to behold,

And in each other, a story yet to be told,

So let us live our lives with purpose and grace,

And make the most of this fleeting time and place.

• 157 •

# 28. Nourishment's Nexus: The Interplay of Food and Wellness

Verdant greens and fruits of hue most bright
Provide sustenance for bodies to thrive.
But oft we stray from diet that is right,
And suffer ill effects that come alive.

Methinks, the nourishment of mortal frame
Is not a trifle to be cast aside,
But rather, crucial to our very aim
Of health and longevity, as a guide.

Forsooth, the balance of our humors' flow,
Is paramount in maintaining health,
And diet plays a vital role, we know,
In regulating that which is our wealth.

Thus let us all be mindful of our fare,
And choose with care, for body's sake, to spare.

It is imperative that we consume
Aliments that are rich in vital nutrients
For without them, our bodies shall assume
A state of dysfunction, and its fruits

In the form of maladies, shall manifest
It is thus, our dietary choices should be invested
with utmost discernment and circumspection
Lest we fall prey to illnesses, with no exception

The correlation between diet and wellness
Is indubitable, and cannot be denied
For the food we consume, does nought but express
Our physical and mental state inside

Hence, let us be vigilant, in our dietary choices
For they shall determine our fate, with no voices
In sum, a diet that is balanced and nutritious
Is the key to a life that is harmonious and auspicious

And let us not forget the importance
Of hydration in our daily quest
For water, the elixir of life,
Is essential for bodily rest

In addition to providing energy,
A proper diet also aids in digestion
It helps to rid the body of impurities
And promotes optimal cognition

And yet, despite its obvious benefits,
We often neglect our dietary needs
We indulge in foods that bring us no nutrients

And suffer the consequences with great speed

But let us not despair, for it is never too late
To make a change, and cultivate a healthier state

Let us take a holistic approach,
To nourishing both body and mind
For a well-rounded diet can help us cope
With the stress and challenges we find

It is through the food we eat, we can express
Our commitment to self-care, and nothing less

In conclusion, diet plays an integral role
In maintaining the balance of our whole
Let us choose our food with care and grace
For it is the foundation of a healthy space
Both physically and mentally, let us strive
To make diet a priority in our lives.

# 29. The Concealed Devotion: A Philosophical Exploration of Piety and Compassion

In the shadows of piety, where devotion doth reside,
Lies a heart that longs for the Creator to abide,
But alas, the love for our fellow man is often denied,
As our hearts are clouded by the world's insipid tide.

Though we honor our Creator with fervent zeal,
Our piety remains unseen, a hidden gem,
For the love of our fellow man we cannot feel,
As our knowledge of compassion is not keen.

Though in our souls, a spark of hope remains,
The chance it will be realized is slim,
For the power of love that cannot be feigned,
The price of such, is often too grim.

So let us strive to move closer to love,
For in understanding our fellow human,
We may find a path to the Creator above,
And restore hope in the midst of the mundane.

Let us not judge, but ask ourselves,
To understand human nature better,

For in compassion and love, true piety dwells,
And hope for all, will forever be a treasure.

For it is only through understanding and compassion,
That we can truly honor our Creator's plan.
Let us not be blinded by our own arrogance,
But open our hearts to the suffering of man.

For it is through selfless acts of kindness,
That we can truly fulfill our duty,
To love and care for our fellow man,
And in doing so, find true beauty.

So let us strive to be more compassionate,
And cast aside the shackles of our pride,
For in serving others, we find true liberation,
And in the end, our souls will be sanctified.

So let us not just talk of piety,
But put it into action, in humility.
Let us not just honor the Creator,
But also honor the creation in humility.

For true devotion is not just in words,
But in deeds, that bring love to the world.
It is in loving our fellow man,
That we honor the Creator, and find true worth.

So let us strive to be more compassionate,

And cast aside the shackles of our pride,
For in serving others, we find true liberation,
And in the end, our souls will be sanctified.

For though we may honor our Creator,
And profess our faith with eloquence and fervor,
If our actions do not mirror our words,
Then our piety remains nothing but a charade, a mere shimmer.

But if we can learn to love our fellow man,
And extend compassion and kindness to all,
Then in the eyes of the Creator, we shall stand,
As true servants of love, with hearts that are tall.

For it is not the grandiose acts of devotion,
But the small acts of love, that truly matter,
For they are the ones that show our true emotion,
And bring light to the world, like a beacon.

So let us strive to love, not just profess,
For in love, true piety shall be expressed.

# 30. Nourishment's Nexus: The Interplay of Food and Wellness

Verdant greens and fruits of hue most bright
Provide sustenance for bodies to thrive.
But oft we stray from diet that is right,
And suffer ill effects that come alive.

Methinks, the nourishment of mortal frame
Is not a trifle to be cast aside,
But rather, crucial to our very aim
Of health and longevity, as a guide.

Forsooth, the balance of our humors' flow,
Is paramount in maintaining health,
And diet plays a vital role, we know,
In regulating that which is our wealth.

Thus let us all be mindful of our fare,
And choose with care, for body's sake, to spare.

It is imperative that we consume
Aliments that are rich in vital nutrients
For without them, our bodies shall assume
A state of dysfunction, and its fruits

In the form of maladies, shall manifest
It is thus, our dietary choices should be invested
with utmost discernment and circumspection
Lest we fall prey to illnesses, with no exception

The correlation between diet and wellness
Is indubitable, and cannot be denied
For the food we consume, does nought but express
Our physical and mental state inside

Hence, let us be vigilant, in our dietary choices
For they shall determine our fate, with no voices
In sum, a diet that is balanced and nutritious
Is the key to a life that is harmonious and auspicious

And let us not forget the importance
Of hydration in our daily quest
For water, the elixir of life,
Is essential for bodily rest

In addition to providing energy,
A proper diet also aids in digestion
It helps to rid the body of impurities
And promotes optimal cognition

And yet, despite its obvious benefits,
We often neglect our dietary needs
We indulge in foods that bring us no nutrients

And suffer the consequences with great speed

But let us not despair, for it is never too late
To make a change, and cultivate a healthier state

Let us take a holistic approach,
To nourishing both body and mind
For a well-rounded diet can help us cope
With the stress and challenges we find

It is through the food we eat, we can express
Our commitment to self-care, and nothing less

In conclusion, diet plays an integral role
In maintaining the balance of our whole
Let us choose our food with care and grace
For it is the foundation of a healthy space
Both physically and mentally, let us strive
To make diet a priority in our lives.

# 31. Kwai's Enduring Influence

For kwai endures, its influence not to fade,
A bond between the rich and poor, a symbol true,
A history that will always be remembered, never to be sway'd.
And so, it is served in every household, every abode,
In the matrilineal society of Meghalaya,
Its legacy will endure, for centuries to go.

For kwai is not just a leaf, it is a friend,
A companion on lonely journeys, a comfort for the soul,
And in its presence, even strangers can befriend,
Their bond strengthened by its offering, a goal.
And so it is chewed, in happiness and in grief,
Its influence, a permanent relief.

For kwai raises blood circulation, so they say,
And blesses the body with health, with every chew,
A symbol of the state's hospitality, in every way,
And so it is served, a custom that will always ensue.
In the matrilineal society of Meghalaya,
Kwai will always be served, its legacy will ensconce.

And so, let us raise a leaf of kwai, and view,
Its influence, its tradition, its essence so grand,
A bond between friends, a symbol of equality, so true,

An offering to guests, to kin, to strangers, to all in the land,
In the matrilineal society of Meghalaya,
Where kwai will always stand, a tradition so tall.

# 32. Solace in the Shadows: An Ode to Darkness

In the nascent stage, I was beset with fear,
Of the inky blackness that surrounds me,
But as the hours passed, I came to hold dear,
The solace found in darkness, e'en though it be

A constant companion, never far away,
And though at first it seemed a foe to face,
I came to see it as a guide, to stay
With me through all the trials of life's race

For in the dark, the mind is free to roam,
Unfettered by the distractions of the light,
And in the quiet, I found my true home,
The only song that I could dance to, right.

And so I've come to see that darkness, too,
Is just a part of life, and I'll pursue.

It with acceptance, for it shapes my soul,
And in its depths, my true self is made whole.

For though it may seem bleak, and cold, and drear,
It holds within it secrets, yet to hear.

It is a source of strength, and not of fear,
And in its silent embrace, I hold dear

The beauty of the unknown, and the path
That leads me to my destiny at last.

And so I'll dance within the dark, and sing
A song of praise for all that it can bring.

For in the end, I know that I'll be free,
And darkness will have been the key to me.

And in the end, I'll see that all along,
The darkness was my guide, my shining song.

It showed me how to find my way through life,
And helped me rise above the endless strife.

It taught me to embrace the mystery,
And find my place in this vast tapestry.

And so I'll walk with pride, and head held high,
For in the darkness, I have learned to fly.

And though the night may seem unending, still,
I'll trust in it, and know that all is well.

For though the darkness may obscure the way,
It also leads to a new dawning day.

And so I'll dance with darkness, hand in hand,
And know that it is part of life's grand plan.

And as I journey on through life's dark night,
I'll hold the darkness close, my guiding light.

For in the dark, I've found a sense of peace,
And in the silence, a sense of release.

It's taught me how to find my strength within,
And how to weather life's tumultuous spin.

And so I'll dance with darkness till the end,
For it's my truest friend, my closest kin.

And though the world may see it as a curse,
I'll see it as the universe's verse.

For in the darkness, I have found my way,
And in the end, it'll be with me to stay.

And so I'll sing my song and dance my dance,
For in the darkness, I have found my chance.

And as I dance with darkness, I'll recall
The times I trembled, and the times I'd fall.

But through it all, the darkness held me near,

And wiped away my doubts and all my fear.

It's been my constant guide, my shining star,
And though it may seem dark, it's gone thus far.

And now I'll dance with darkness to the end,
And know that it's my truest and my friend.

It's been my shelter in the raging storms,
And in its silence, I've found my true forms.

So I'll embrace the darkness, and its might,
For it's been my companion in the night.

And as I dance with darkness, I'll be free,
For it's my guide and it's my destiny.

# 33. Simplicitas: A Sonnet on the Pared-Down Path of Minimalism

Simplicity is key, in all we do and say,
A minimalistic approach, a purer way,
To strip away the excess, and find the core,
Of what is true and meaningful, and more.

But in this quest for minimalism, we find,
That less is oft a double-edged sword, designed,
To cut away the dross, and leave the gold,
But also to leave nought but emptiness, cold.

For in our search for purity, we see,
That oft we lose the beauty, in the spare,
And in our zeal for simplification,
We find ourselves in destitution, bare.

Thus, true minimalism is not a state,
Of pared-down being, but a delicate balance,
Of keeping only that which truly matters,
And letting go of all that hinders, chancers.

It is a journey, not a destination,
A path of self-discovery and cultivation,

Away from material excess, and towards,
A state of inner peace, and mind-body accord.

It is a way of living, that embraces,
The beauty and the simplicity of life's spaces,
Emptying the mind of all but what is true,
And finding contentment in the smallest dew.

Minimalism is not a lack of something,
But a process of subtraction, thus a bringing,
Of the essential elements of life,
And a focus on what truly brings content and strife.

It is a discipline, that requires practice,
To learn to distinguish, the noise from the message,
And to find the beauty, in the simplest things,
And to discard the rest, as meaningless.

In this way, minimalism becomes a path,
To a deeper understanding, of our own selves,
And the world around us, and it's aftermath,
A way to find true happiness, and wealth.

So let us embrace minimalism, as a guide,
To living a simpler, and more authentic life,
And let us find, in its simplicity,
A way to true fulfillment, and end of strife.

Minimalism is not just about material possessions,

But also about the thoughts and emotions we hold,
It is about letting go of all obsession,
And finding peace in the present, as we are told.

It is a way to live a more meaningful life,
By focusing on what truly matters and bring joy,
It is a way to find balance in the midst of life's strife,
And to let go of what only serves to annoy.

It is a way to declutter our mind,
And to simplify our thoughts and beliefs,
It is about living with intention and not in blind,
And to find true purpose and achieve relief.

Minimalism is a journey, not a destination,
A path of self-discovery and liberation,
It is a way of living, that embraces
The beauty and the simplicity of life's spaces.

So let us embrace minimalism, as a guide,
To living a simpler, and more authentic life,
And let us find, in its simplicity,
A way to true fulfillment, and end of strife.

# 34. Hazy Visions: A Sonnet on the Consequences of Inebriation

In the morning light, my vision obscured by a misty veil,
A consequence of last night's indulgent imbibing,
I lament the choices that led to this tale,
Of a throbbing headache, and a spirit of pleading.

Like a habitual inebriate's perspective on life's despair,
I find myself in this abyss of remorse,
The decisions made, the paths that led me there,
All pointing to one thing: I did not endorse

The standards set by morality, virtue, and self-regard,
I allowed my actions to be dictated by drink,
And now, in this foggy state, I am unable to discard
The truth that I am nothing but a fragile link.

All that remains,
Is to make amends and hope that in this haze,
Illumination will arrive and bring change.
And reshape my path, out of this drunken maze.

For it is through self-reflection and atonement,
That we may rise above our base inclinations,

And find the light that guides us towards redemption,
Away from the darkness of our drunken sensations.

# 35. The Illusion of Grandeur: A Meditation on Materialism

In the midst of my unyielding pursuit of lucre and prestige,
My intellect was clouded by the siren song of material acquisition,
And I came to realize that beneath the veneer of success,
I was but a commoner, dressed in tattered garments.

Despite the wealth and fame that I had amassed,
They brought me nothing but emptiness and melancholy,
For deep within my psyche, I remained unfulfilled,
A mere shadow of my aspirations.

But still I clung to my illusions of grandeur,
Chasing the illusions of wealth and fame,
Forgetting that true worth is not found in material gain,
But in the integrity of one's inner being.

And so in the end, I found myself alone,
A victim of my own avarice and arrogance,
Trapped in a world where true happiness is elusive,
A prisoner of my own despair and defeat.

But as I reflect upon my past mistakes,
I see the path to redemption and self-awareness,
To shed the shackles of my own desires and wants,
And find true fulfillment in the inner self.

For in the end, it is not wealth or fame that brings happiness,
But the cultivation of virtue and wisdom within,
To lead a life of purpose and meaning,
And to find solace in the simple things.

So I vow to strive towards self-improvement,
To cast aside the trappings of materialism,
And to seek true fulfillment in the depths of my being,
So that I may transcend my plebeian existence.

For in the end, true wealth lies not in gold or jewels,
But in the richness of the human spirit.

And as I journey on this path of self-discovery,
I realize that true success is not measured by fame or wealth,
But by the way one lives their life with integrity,
And the impact one leaves on the world.

For in the end, true greatness is not attained through power or wealth,
But through the cultivation of compassion and empathy,
To be a force for good in the world,
And to leave a legacy of kindness and generosity.

So I pledge to live my life with purpose and intention,
To strive for personal growth and self-improvement,
To be a beacon of hope and inspiration,
And to leave a mark on the world that will be remembered.

For in the end, it is not the material things that matter,
But the way we lived our lives and the memories we leave behind.

# 36. The Lament of the Timeless Bibliophile

In this age of modernity, I doth despise
The digitized tomes that clutter up the mind
For in their screens, true beauty doth not rise
But rather, leaves the soul in a bind

In contemplation of the ancient past,
I oft do muse upon the fabled tomes
That lay within the libraries amassed
And ponder on the knowledge they contain

Ah, were I gifted with the power to time travel
And journey to the libraries of old
To peruse the scrolls and unravel
The secrets that within them are told

To stand within the halls of Alexandria's grandeur
And read the works of scholars long since passed
To marvel at the Library of Pergamum's splendor
And in the words of Homer be amassed

But alas, such fantastical dreams remain
For the power to time travel is a vain

Yet still, the longing for the knowledge of old

Burns bright within my heart and soul
And though the means to attain it may be cold
I shall strive to make my goal

To seek out understanding and truth
In every age, in every youth.

For though the ancient libraries may be lost
Their wisdom still remains
In fragments, scattered at any cost
For future generations to attain

And though the physical tomes may be gone
Their essence still remains
Through translations and digital dawn
For us to know and gain

But it is not just the ancient past
That holds knowledge to behold
For every era and culture amassed
Has stories to be told

Thus, my quest for understanding
Is not limited to one time
But encompasses the expanding
Wisdom of humanity's climb

For in the pursuit of knowledge, there is no end
And I shall strive until the very end.

And though I may not physically see
The ancient libraries of old
I shall not let that hindrance be
A barrier to the knowledge to be told

For the digital age has brought
New means to access the past
Through digitized texts, knowledge is sought
And the wisdom of the ancients can be amassed

And though the physical experience may be lacking
The substance of the knowledge remains
For in the digital realm, it keeps on tracking
And it eternally sustains

So let us not lament the loss of the past
But rather, embrace the knowledge that will last
And in this digital age, let us strive
To expand our understanding and come alive.

And let us not forget that knowledge does not reside
solely in ancient libraries or digital realm alone
but also in the oral traditions and cultural pride
of different communities and their own.

So let us not confine ourselves to one source
But broaden our perspective and explore
For in the diverse knowledge we can endorse

Lies the potential for a richer understanding and more.

Let us not limit ourselves to the written word
But also seek out the knowledge of the unheard
For in their stories and traditions
Lies a wealth of wisdom and visions

So let us strive to visit all libraries, both ancient and new
For in them lies the key to a richer understanding of the world and the
truth.

And as we journey on this quest for knowledge,
Let us not forget the importance of critical thinking,
For it is through questioning and analysis,
That we can truly understand and begin linking

The pieces of the puzzle together,
To form a clearer picture of the world,
And in this way, we can gain a better
Understanding of our place in it, unfurled.

For knowledge is not just about acquiring information,
But also about how we interpret and use it,
And in this way, we can strive for a greater liberation
From ignorance and towards a more enlightened pursuit.

So let us visit all libraries, ancient and new,
And in them, let us seek the truth and pursue.

# 37. The Drunkard's Dilemma: An Exploration of Free Will and Destiny

Whilst traveling in a maxi-cab, I chanced upon a drunkard , Bahnah Bhoi his name,

Who incessantly questioned me about my attire, and my usage of lip cream,

He confided in me of his past as a bodyguard of a parish priest in his hometown,

And spoke of his bitter life, choosing whiskey over water,

And tobacco rolls in place of sustenance.

But even in his drunken state, he maintained a semblance of self-preservation,

Eating vegetables for vitamins, and meats for protein.

Then he began to rattle on,

About the 2023 General Election,

And how he was paid with a mere five hundred rupees and a bottle of whiskey,

To cast his vote for a friend in the upcoming month.


All of which is but a mere illusion of control, in a world of chaos and misery,

Where our actions are predetermined and controlled by fate,

And in the end, we are all but mere puppets in the grand scheme of things.

But as I listened to his words, I couldn't help but ponder,
On the true nature of free will and destiny,
Are we truly in control of our actions and thoughts,
Or are we just mere pawns in a cosmic game, played by the deity.

And as I pondered, I came to a realization,
That perhaps it is not the destination that matters,
But the journey, the choices we make, and the lessons we learn,
That shape the course of our lives, and the fate of our souls.

So let us not be held captive,
By the illusions of control and fate,
For in the end, it is our choices, that truly shape our destination,
And give meaning to our existence, before it's too late.

For in the end, it is not fate, but our choices,
That determine the course of our lives,
It is our actions and thoughts, that give voice,
To the purpose and meaning, that thrives.

So let us not be swayed, by the illusions of control,
For in the end, it is our choices, that shape our role,
In this grand scheme of things, that is life,
And give meaning to our existence, in the midst of strife.

For though we may be but mere puppets,
In the grand scheme of things,
It is our choices, that make us true kings,

And give us the power to transcend, and to sing.

So let us embrace our choices,
And make the most of our lives,
For in the end, it is our choices,
That give meaning to our existence, and to our lives.

# 38. Existence in the Boundless Cosmos: A Sonnet on the Search for Life and Consciousness in the Universe

Is there any existence in the disparate realms of the vast expanse of this
boundless cosmos?
Or are we but mere specks in the grand scheme,
Alone in our struggles and our pain?

Does consciousness exist beyond our earthly sphere,
In forms unknown and yet to be discerned?
Or are we the highest form, the apex of evolution,
With naught but silence and emptiness to be learned?

The mysteries of the universe are vast and deep,
And may forever elude our understanding,
But still we search and strive to go beyond,
To seek the truth and find a higher landing.

Perhaps in the vast expanse of space,
There is life, in forms both known and strange,
And though the quest may be a difficult race,
We must continue to seek and to change.

For the quest for knowledge is a never-ending tale,
And the answers to our questions may be elusive, frail.

But in the quest for truth and understanding,
We find purpose and meaning in our being,
For to question and to seek is human nature,
And the pursuit of knowledge is worth the striving.

And though the answers may be hard to find,
And the path may be long and winding,
We must not let the doubts and fears bind,
Our hearts and minds from climbing.

For in the vast expanse of the universe,
There may be life, in forms yet to be discovered,
And though the journey may be perilous,
We must continue to seek and uncover.

For the quest for knowledge is a noble cause,
And in the search for answers, we evolve.

And though the answers may not be clear,
We must not give up, for the truth is always near.

And though the universe may seem cold and dark,
With no sign of life and no answers to be found,
We must not lose hope or fall apart,
For the quest for knowledge is a journey profound.

For in the vast expanse of the universe,
There may be life, in forms yet to be seen,
And though the journey may be difficult and diverse,
We must continue to seek and to dream.

For in the quest for truth and understanding,
We find ourselves and our place in the grand scheme,
And though the answers may be hard to comprehending,
We must continue to search, to learn and to redeem.

For the quest for knowledge is a lifelong pursuit,
And the answers to our questions may be elusive, but it's worth the fruit.

And as we journey through the vast expanse,
We may find that the answers are not so far,
For in the depths of our own existence,
We may find that the answers are not so hard.

For the search for knowledge is not just in the stars,
But in the depths of our own hearts,
And though the universe may be vast and far,
The answers to our questions may be closer than we thought.

So let us not be daunted by the vast expanse,
Or the unknown and the unseen,
For in the quest for truth and understanding,
We are fulfilling our true humanity.

For the quest for knowledge is not just a pursuit,
But a journey of self-discovery that is worth the root.

# 39. The Melancholic Masquerade: A Sonnet on the Bitterness of Existence

The acrimonious essence of existence oft assails,
A scourge of lamentation that beguiles the psyche.
With tribulations and misfortunes that assail,
The piquancy of merriment fades and all the while

I am constrained to affect a facade of joy,
A charade of felicity to exhibit.
Yet all the while, my heart is wracked with rancor,
And all my days are spent in melancholic despair.

O life, thy bitter potion is arduous to endure,
With every sip, my soul doth faint and tire.
But still, I'll endeavor to find a shimmer of hope,
And aspire to find solace in the inferno.

So let me endure this acrid chalice with poise,
And harbor the expectation of redemption in a superior realm.

For though the world may seem a bleak and dreary place,
And all around is shrouded in a veil of sorrow,
I'll not succumb to hopelessness and despair,
But strive to find the light that shines beyond tomorrow.

For life, though bitter, holds within its grasp
The potential for beauty, love and truth.
Though pain and suffering may come to pass,
They serve to strengthen and to guide our youth.

So let us not bemoan our mortal fate,
But take the bitter with the sweet, and learn.
For in this fleeting life, we can create
A legacy of love and light, to burn.

And when our time on earth is at an end,
We'll find eternal peace, and call it friend.

# 40. The Anti-Heroine's Anthem: The Resilience of Venus in the War Against the Meaning of Life

With rancor and retribution as her anthem,
She stands resolute, a pharos of fortitude and puissance,
No longer the damsel who would take a subservient stance,
But a formidable presence, both diurnal and nocturnal.

She's the anti-heroine of our era,
A dissident with a raison d'etre, a combatant for amor,
She's the orator of the shattered and the forlorn,
A divinity of the downtrodden, sent from on high.

She sings of the agony and the hurt we all endure,
Of the cicatrices that we bear, and the struggles we've surmounted,
But all is for naught, for love is but an illusion,
A fleeting mirage in a world of endless suffering.

For in this world, we are but mere mortals,
Bound by the shackles of mortality,
Forever in search of an eternal portal,
To escape the reality of our finality.

But still, Venus, our anti-heroine,
Fights on, in a war against the meaning of life,
For in the end, all is but a futile dream,
And love, but a fleeting, bittersweet respite.

And though her quest may be in vain,
We shall forever remember her name,
For in her struggle, we gain
The courage to face the eternal game.

And though her quest may be in vain,
We shall forever remember her name,
For in her struggle, we gain
The courage to face the eternal game.

For in this world, we are but mere mortals,
Bound by the shackles of mortality,
Forever in search of an eternal portal,
To escape the reality of our finality.

But Venus, our anti-heroine,
Refuses to accept this fate,
She fights for love, and for a dream,
That may be but a fleeting state.

For in this war against the meaning of life,
She reminds us to never give up the fight,
To never accept the endless strife,
And to always hold on to the light.

So here's to Venus, our anti-heroine,
A valiant warrior in a war against the meaning of life,
For in the end, all is but a futile dream,
And love, but a fleeting, bittersweet respite.

And though the war may seem unending,
And the quest for love may seem in vain,
Venus, our anti-heroine, is never bending,
She fights on, with passion and disdain.

For in this world of endless suffering,
She reminds us of the beauty of love,
Of the hope that it can be an offering,
A guiding light, from above.

And though the struggle may be hard,
And the road may be long,
She reminds us to keep our hearts guarded,
And to hold on to what is right and strong.

So let us take inspiration from Venus,
Our anti-heroine, in the quest for love,
For in the end, it is the only purpose,
That elevates our souls above.

And as we walk this mortal coil,
With Venus, our anti-heroine by our side,
We shall face the world's turmoil,

With a heart full of love and pride.

For in the end, love is what endures,
A beacon of hope in the darkest of days,
It is the light that always assures,
That there's a better way to pave.

And Venus, our anti-heroine,
Reminds us to never give up the fight,
To never lose sight of what is true,
And to always hold on to the light.

So let us take her as our guide,
In this quest for love and meaning,
For in her struggle, we shall find,
The courage to keep on leaning.

And in the end, we shall transcend,
And realize that love is the only end.

# 41. U Lumsohpetbneng

The Khasis tell of a world created by God,
A place of beauty where 16 families trod,
In heaven they lived, but longed for earth's allure,
So God allowed seven huts, hynniew-trep, to endure.

They settled on earth, happy and content,
But soon were tempted by an evil intent,
To cut down the Golden Ladder, a mighty tree,
On Lumdiengiei, connecting heaven and sea.

They thought its branches blocked the Sun's warm rays,
But each day, the tree was whole, in wondrous ways.
A bird named Phreit revealed the secret truth,
A tiger licked the cuts, in nocturnal youth.

So axes were turned, blades facing out,
And the tiger's tongue was hurt, without a doubt.
The tree was felled, but darkness fell on earth,
A Dorbar was called, for a new plan's birth.

They pleaded with God, for sunlight to return,
And a rooster stepped forward, his life to burn.
God accepted the sacrifice, and the Sun shone,
And the rooster was gifted with a morning moan.

But as the Cock crows each dawn, a cryptic note,
A reminder of the past, and what it wrote.
For in the cutting of the Ladder, true sin,
The Khasis lost connection with heaven within.

And though the Sun may shine, and life goes on,
The Khasis still long for the Golden Ladder, gone.
For in its loss, they lost a piece of themselves,
And in redemption, they seek to regain wealth.

But as they search for what was lost, they'll find,
A new connection, a different kind.
For though the Ladder may be gone, a path remains,
And in it, the Khasis will find new gains.

So let the Cock's cry be a somber call,
A reminder of the past, and what befell.
For in its loss, a new journey begins,
And the Khasis will find redemption within.

# 42. The Perspicacity of Fate: A Sonnet on Personal Accountability

Presently, ere thou dost pledge thyself to a life of despondent meniality, attend with sagacity.

I have imparted this truism, as many of us perceive ourselves as beholden to the vicissitudes of reality.

We are fraught with melancholy as a consequence.

Nay, nay, and nay. Thou must assume accountability for EVERY bloody occurrence that transpires in thy life.

Not because thou art a submissive simpleton, but because thou art a resolute and formidable individual who comprehends their agency as creators of their reality and fate.

If thou resort to blame or victimhood in any manifestation, thou signal to the deities that thou art a craven and subservient individual, and shalt be treated accordingly. Refrain from such actions.

But heed not to despair, for with this accountability comes power,
To shape and mold thy life, to rise above the dreary hour.
With steadfast determination and an unyielding will,
Thou shalt transcend the shackles of fate and climb the summit still.

So cast off thy doubts and fears, and take control of thy fate,
For thou art not a victim, but the master of thy own state.
With each step and every choice, thou shalt shape thy destiny,

And rise above the fray, a true sovereign of thy entity.

So heed my words and heed them well, for they are not in vain,
For with them thou shalt find the strength to break free from the
chain.
And though the path may be long and hard, fear not, for thou art
strong,
With perseverance and resolve, thou shalt right all that is wrong.

And in the end, when all is said and done,
Thou shalt stand tall, victorious, having won.
For thou hast taken control of thy fate,
And shaped thy destiny, with a will unbreakable and great.

But remember, dear friend, this journey is not done,
For every day, new challenges will come.
But fear not, for with each one, thou shalt grow,
And become a being of strength, wisdom, and flow.

So heed my words, and heed them well,
For they hold the key to a life that will excel.
Embrace your agency, and take the reins,
For a life of fulfillment, power, and gains.

And let this be a reminder, to always strive,
To shape your reality, and truly come alive.

But also remember, dear friend, to be kind,
To yourself and others, for in compassion, we truly bind.

For in this life, as we shape our fate,
We must also remember to nurture and create.
Create love, create joy, create peace,
For in giving, we truly find release.

So heed my words and heed them well,
For they hold the key to a life that will excel.
Embrace your agency, take the reins,
But also remember to love, and to heal.

For in this balance, dear friend, you will find,
A life fulfilled, a heart open and kind.
And in this state, you will truly shine,
A beacon of light, in a world that is often blind.

So heed my words, and heed them well,
For they hold the key to a life that will excel.

# 43. Perseverance in Adversity: A Sonnet on the Resilience of Cancer Patients

The malignancy of cancer's scourge,
A pathogen that ravages the flesh,
A foe that oft does leave one feeling purged,
And drained of all one's vital energy and zest.

The struggle of the patients oft beset,
By pain and fear and uncertainty,
Their bodies wracked by treatments that have met,
With the disease in bitter enmity.

But despite the trials and tribulations,
The patients show a strength that is quite rare,
A fortitude that in their tribulations,
Is born of will, and courage, and great care.

For though the cancer may consume the body,
The spirit remains unbroken and unshoddy.

Their perseverance is a testament,
To the human spirit's unyielding zest,
Their strength in face of suffering and bent,
A shining light in darkest of the mess.

Though fate may deal a hand of tragedy,
The patients rise above with dignity,
Their resilience in the face of malady,
An inspiration for all humanity.

For though the cancer may ravage the frame,
The spirit, unbroken, remains the same,
A testament to the will to survive,
And the innate resilience to strive.

And though the journey may be long and hard,
The patients' strength serves as a shining guard,
A beacon of hope in the darkest night,
A reminder that we too can take flight.

So let us honor the strength of these souls,
Whose struggles have made them truly whole,
For in their journey, we see our own,
And the strength to overcome, we have grown.

For though the cancer may ravage the form,
The patients' will to live will never be torn,
Their determination to fight and survive,
Is a testament to the human drive.

Their journey through the valley of the shadow,
Is one of strength and courage, not of sorrow,
For they have faced the beast with heads held high,

And in their struggle, we can see the why.

The why of life, the why of hope, the why of love,
The patients' fight has shown us all above,
The beauty in the struggle, in the pain,
The beauty in the will to live again.

Theirs is a journey of the human spirit,
One of resilience, and of merit,
Theirs is a story of the human soul,
A story of the will to make us whole.

So let us honor the strength of these souls,
Whose struggles have made them truly whole,
For in their journey, we see our own,
And the strength to overcome, we have grown.

For though the cancer may seem like a curse,
It serves to strengthen and to make us better,
To teach us about life, and its purpose,
And to remind us that we are all just letters.

Letters in the great story of humanity,
Each one with its own struggles and its own pain,
But through it all, we find unity,
In the fight to live, and to live again.

The cancer patients' journey is a reminder,
Of the strength and resilience of the human mind,

That even in the darkest days, one can find,
The will to live, and to be kind.

So let us honor the strength of these souls,
Whose struggles have made them truly whole,
For in their journey, we see our own,
And the strength to overcome, we have grown.

And in the end, when our journey is through,
We will look back and see all we've been through,
And find that the struggles we faced along the way,
Were the very things that helped us find our way.

And though the cancer may be a harsh test,
It serves to teach us what is truly best,
To find the strength within, to rise above,
To find the meaning of true self-love.

For the cancer patients' journey is a path,
Of self-discovery, of healing, and of growth,
A path that leads to a deeper understanding,
Of what it means to truly live, and to be whole.

For though the cancer may be a cruel fate,
It serves to teach us to appreciate,
The beauty in the struggle, the strength in the fight,
And the will to live, with all our might.

So let us honor the strength of these souls,

Whose struggles have made them truly whole,
For in their journey, we see our own,
And the strength to overcome, we have grown.

And in the end, when our journey is through,
We will look back and see all we've been through,
And find that the struggles we faced along the way,
Were the very things that helped us find our way.

# 44. Perilous Prognostication: A Sonnet of Cherishing Moments

Prognostication, a perilous pursuit,
A quest to predict the future's shape,
A moot endeavor that engenders hurt,
And suffering, when reality doth escape

Our expectations for life and those around,
But if we lay aside this futile chase,
And focus on cherishing each moment found,
We shall find peace and resilience in our grace.

For as George Pransky hath wisely said,
The truth of living in the present,
Is the key to happiness, and the dread
Of future's unknown, shall be lessened.

Thus, let us lay aside prognostication,
And cherish each moment, with exultation.

Indeed, prognostication is a trap,
That leads to nought but worry and mishap,
For the future is a mystery, unseen,
And trying to predict it, is a fruitless dream.

But if we learn to live in the present,
And cherish each moment, as it is meant,
We shall find a sense of peace and serenity,
And the ability to face adversity.

For in the present, we find the truth,
Of life and its beauty, and the proof,
That happiness is not in tomorrow,
But in the now, that we must follow.

So let us lay aside prognostication,
And embrace the present, with elation.

Indeed, prognostication is a curse
That leads to nothing but anxiety and remorse,
For the future is a realm unknown,
And trying to predict it, is a futile drone.

But if we learn to live in the now,
And cherish each moment, without a vow,
We shall find a sense of tranquility
And the ability to face adversity.

For in the present, we find the key
To happiness, and the way to be,
Content with what is, and not what will be,
And in this acceptance, true liberty.

So let us lay aside prognostication,
And live in the present, with liberation.

Indeed, prognostication is a vain pursuit,
A futile endeavor that bears no fruit,
For the future is ever-changing and uncertain,
And trying to predict it, is a futile burden.

But if we learn to live in the moment,
And cherish each day, as it is sent,
We shall find a sense of serenity,
And the ability to face adversity.

For in the present, we find the truth
Of life, and its beauty, and the proof
That happiness is not in tomorrow,
But in the now, that we must follow.

So let us lay aside prognostication,
And embrace the present, with exultation.

# 45. The Sagacious Mind: A Sonnet of Imagination and Perception

Lo, man doth possess the cognitive aptitude

To conjure images within his mind's eye,

Imagination's gift hath led to creation

Of efficacious machines and novel designs,

A trait that sets our kind apart from others.

But thoughts, though fair, can oft be fraught with danger,

For they are but approximations, fleeting,

That poorly mirror truth and reality.

Thus, one must not ascribe them undue trust,

For to do so is to play a perilous game.

Instead, let us cultivate a wise relation

With the profound and hidden sagacity

That lies beneath the surface of our thoughts,

Where true potential and success doth lie.

In sooth, to rely solely on the mind's eye

Is to embrace a narrow, limited scope,

And oft leads to a state of cognitive stupor,

Where one becomes a prisoner of the mind's trope.

Thus, we must strive to transcend the mortal coil

And tap into the eternal, cosmic whole

By seeking out the wisdom that doth lie

Beyond the realm of mere thoughts and mortal toil.
For only through this quest for higher truth
Can we unlock the secrets of the soul,
And shed the shackles of our earthly youth
To reach a state of being whole and whole.
So let us not be slaves to our own mind,
But seek the wisdom that doth lay enshrined.

Indeed, the mind's potential is vast and grand,
But oft it is constrained by mortal bands.
It's crucial that we strive to comprehend
The vast expanse that lies beyond our strands.
For only through the pursuit of higher thought
Can we transcend the limits of our ken
And tap into the cosmic, eternal sought
That lies beyond the realm of mortal men.
Thus, let us not be content with mortal fate
But seek to rise above our earthly state
And reach for the stars, beyond the pearly gate
To grasp the secrets of the universe and state.
For only in this quest for higher truth
Can we unlock the secrets of our youth.

In sooth, the mind is like a boundless sea,
With depths unknown, and mysteries to be.
But oft, we let the waves of thought run free,
Without a compass, or a map, or key.
Thus, it is crucial that we navigate
The vast expanse of thought with care and skill,

To chart a course that will elevate
Our being, and our will, to greater still.
For only through a journey of the mind
Can we unlock the secrets of the self,
And understand the truths that we must find
To reach a state of being, far from pelf.
So let us not be slaves to our own thought,
But seek the wisdom that doth lie, unsought.

# 46. The Fasting Conundrum: A Sonnet on Intermittent Abstinence

The practice of abstaining from sustenance,
Intermittently, doth provoke inquiry;
For though the fast may bring some recompense,
Its true worth and efficacy doth vary.

The human body, a complex machine,
Requires nourishment for optimal function;
And though the fast may bring some semblance of lean,
Its long-term effects remain in question.

The fast may bring some weight loss, it is true,
But at what cost to one's overall health?
For if the fast doth lead to nutrient dearth,
The body's systems may suffer stealth.

Thus, one must weigh the pros and cons with care,
And consult with a physician, ere they dare.

The practice of abstaining from sustenance,
Intermittently, doth raise ethical questions;
For though the fast may bring some recompense,
Its true worth and efficacy doth remain uncertain.

The human organism, a complex entity,
Requires nourishment for optimal functioning;
And though the fast may bring some semblance of leanness,
Its long-term effects remain a subject of speculation.

The fast may bring some weight loss, it is true,
But at what cost to one's overall well-being?
For if the fast doth lead to nutrient deprivation,
The body's systems may suffer deleterious consequences.

Thus, one must weigh the pros and cons with circumspection,
And consult with a medical professional, ere they embark on such a
regimen.

And though the fast may bring some mental clarity,
It's important to remember that it's not a panacea;
For the mind and body, both must work in harmony,
To achieve true balance and serenity.

The fast may bring some temporary relief,
But it's important to consider the bigger picture;
For true health and wellness is a lifelong pursuit,
And requires a holistic approach and stricture.

Thus, when considering intermittent fasting,
One must take a holistic perspective;
And weigh the benefits and drawbacks, testing
Before committing to such an endeavor.

For though the fast may bring some fleeting gain,
It's important to remember, health is wealth and true wealth is holistic
in nature, not just physical.

And as we strive for optimal health,
It's essential to remember one thing;
That balance is key, and moderation is wealth,
For true health is not just about what we bring.

For the body is not just a physical form,
But a composite of mind, body and soul;
And true health is a balance of all,
With none left out or feeling whole.

Thus, when considering intermittent fasting,
One must take a holistic approach;
And weigh the benefits against the costs,
Before committing to such a encroach.

For though the fast may bring some temporary gain,
True health is a journey, not just a destination.
One must find balance and harmony, to maintain,
And live a life that is fulfilling and filled with satisfaction.

And as we journey towards optimal health,
It's important to remember that the path is unique;
For every individual has their own wealth
Of needs and goals, and what works for one may not work for another.

Intermittent fasting may be beneficial,
For some, but not for all. It's important to listen
To one's own body and seek professional guidance,
Before embarking on any such discipline.

For though the fast may bring some temporary gain,
It's essential to consider the long-term effects;
And ensure that one's overall well-being will not be in vain.

In conclusion, when it comes to intermittent fasting,
One must approach it with caution and care,
And seek professional advice before embarking on this endeavor.

# 47. The Prodigious Squander: A Sonnet on Acceptance

We squander prodigious quantities of vital energy
In the pursuit of acceptance, a futile quest,
An innate predisposition, our primal drive,
To evade predation, now a thing of the past, at rest.

Solace can be attained, though not without sacrifice,
When we reconcile with the inevitability
Of rejection, a bitter and painful price,
But fortunately, this acceptance brings lucidity.

With this realization, we extricate
The consternation from our psyche and acclimate
To the new paradigm, and willingly participate
In the possibility of appearing as a buffoon, our fate.

This acceptance, this power, is an emblem of sovereignty,
A newfound strength, in the face of adversity.

Thus, we must learn to relinquish
The need for acceptance and validation,
For it is a fruitless endeavor,
That leads to nothing but frustration.

Instead, let us strive to be true

To ourselves, and our inner selves,
For in this authenticity, we shall renew
Our strength and find true wealth.

Let us not fear rejection or disdain,
For they are but illusions, fleeting and vain,
But embrace them with equanimity,
And in this acceptance, true authority.

So let us not waste our energy
In the pursuit of acceptance, but be free.

And in this newfound liberty,
We shall find the courage to be,
Unencumbered by the need for conformity,
And free from the shackles of society.

For in embracing our individuality,
We shall gain true authority,
And in this authenticity,
We shall find true humility.

Thus, let us not be swayed by the crowd,
But stand firm in our own individuality, proud,
For in this, we shall find true power,
And the strength to face any hour.

So let us not fear rejection or disdain,
But embrace them with equanimity, and gain.

And in this acceptance of our true selves,
We shall find the courage to pursue our wealths,
Unshackled by the need for validation,
And free to chart our own course, without hesitation.

For in embracing our innate predisposition,
We shall find true liberation,
From the constraints of societal imposition,
And the freedom to be true to our own vocation.

Thus, let us not squander our vitality,
In the pursuit of acceptance, a vain reality,
But instead, let us strive to be true,
To ourselves and our inner selves, in authenticity.

So let us embrace the inevitability
Of rejection, and find solace in our clarity.

# 48. Ethereal Affection: A Sonnet of Unfeigned Beauty

Unfeigned affection, a rarity sublime,
That dwells in realms ethereal and transcendent,
A beauty ineffable, beyond all time,
Worth embracing, to feel connection and resplendent.

We are united, bound inextricably,
But in the corporeal realm, we stand apart,
Discrete entities, in our singularity,
Collectives, clans, kinships, in our own heart.

Adoration, deference, solicitude,
Qualified always in this terrestrial sphere,
No one adores, they cherish what is viewed
As utilitarian, cease to be, and disappear.

This principle, connects us equitably,
Embrace it, and heartbreak shall not be, ultimately.

And so, let us strive to find
This rare and precious thing,
Unfeigned affection of the mind,
A beauty that is beyond all earthly being.

For in its embrace, we shall transcend

The limitations of the mortal plane,
And find a connection that shall never end,
A love that is ethereal, and most humane.

And though in the physical realm we may part,
Our connection shall remain, in the heart
For unfeigned affection is eternal,
A love that shall forever be, most infernal.

So let us cherish this rarity sublime,
And find connection, ethereal and divine.

Indeed, unfeigned affection is a treasure,
A wealth beyond measure,
That dwells in realms ethereal and sublime,
And brings a sense of transcendence, that is prime.

For in its embrace, we find a connection,
A bond that is beyond all comprehension,
A beauty that is ineffable, and pure,
A love that shall forever endure.

But in this mortal realm, it is hard to find,
For often it is masked by the mundane,
And lost in the noise of the mind,
Forged by societal pressures, most profane.

But let us strive to find this treasure,
And embrace it, with unfeigned pleasure.

For unfeigned affection is a rare gem,
That shines with a light, that is most dim
In this world of superficiality and pretence,
But in its presence, we find true essence.

It is a connection that is beyond words,
A feeling that is most sublime and absurd,
A beauty that is ineffable, and rare,
A love that is eternal, and beyond compare.

But to find this treasure, we must look within,
And shed the layers of the superficial skin,
For unfeigned affection is a state of being,
That can only be found, when we stop the fleeing.

So let us strive to find this gem so rare,
And embrace it with a love that is most fair.

# 49. Verbal Labyrinth: A Sonnet of Complexity

In efforts to ensure my missive's flight
I disrupt the network's flow and ebb,
And in the local signal find a blight
That forces them to take a sneakernet web.

Forsooth, my words must reach their intended ears,
Though I employ a lexicon arcane,
With rhymes as intricate as chrysanthemers
And syntax oft as labyrinthine.

But let not this discourage thee, fair friend,
For in this verse doth lie a deeper sense,
A hidden message that doth transcend
The boundaries of common eloquence.

So let us revel in this verbal dance,
And in its complexities, enhance.

And though the path to understanding may
Be fraught with lexical enigmas, stay
Resolute, for in this sonnet's lay
Lies meaning deep and secrets yet to say.

With each verse, let us delve deeper still

Into the layers of this linguistic thrill
For though the words may challenge and test,
The beauty of this verse is truly blessed.

So let us navigate this lexical sea
With courage and with curiosity,
For hidden treasures are there to be
Found in the complexity.

And when at last the message is unfurled
We'll marvel at the beauty of this world
That lies within the depths of language curled.

With each verse, let the language unfurl
And reveal the depths of the poet's world
For though the words may seem abstruse and unfurled
They hold within them secrets yet to be unfurled.

Let us not fear the complexity,
But embrace it with a heart full of glee,
For in its depths lies poetry,
A beauty that is meant to be free.

So let us take this journey, hand in hand
And explore the realm of language grand,
And in its depths, let us understand
The power of words, both simple and grand.

And when our journey comes to an end,

We'll look back, and see how far we've wended.

# 50. Eminence Arisen: A Sonnet of Self-Determination

Eminence, akin to verdant growth or spawn

Of simian progeny, doth not arise

As an inherent trait, but rather, drawn

From human artifice, a construct to size.

But lo, this is not a scourge, but rather boon,

For in the crafting of our own esteem,

We kindle the flame our ancestors have swooned,

And in the embers, find our significance gleam.

Indeed, eminence is not bestowed,

But a product of our own actions and thoughts,

Forged in the fires of our own abode,

And shaped by the struggles that life has brought.

But let us not see this as a curse,

But rather an opportunity,

To craft our own significance, and immerse

Ourselves in the pursuit of our own destiny.

For in the crafting of our own esteem,

We find the power to transcend,

The limitations of our mortal being,

And find a purpose that is most grand.

For eminence is not a gift from fate,
But a product of our own will and grit,
Forged through determination, and the weight
Of struggles, that we must bear and admit.

But let us not despair, nor be forlorn,
For this is an opportunity,
To shape our own destiny, and be reborn,
And find significance, in our own society.

For in the crafting of our own esteem,
We find the power to transcend,
The limitations of our mortal being,
And find a purpose that is most grand.

For eminence is not a birthright,
But a product of our own efforts and might,
Forged through perseverance and insight
And the ability to see beyond the blight.

But let us not lament nor implore,
For this is an opportunity,
To create our own significance, and soar
And find purpose in our own destiny.

For in the crafting of our own esteem,
We find the power to transcend,
The limitations of our mortal being,

And find a purpose that is most grand.

Eminence, a product of our own accord,
Forged in the furnace of life's rigor,
A construct of human artifice, outpoured
Through effort, determination, and vigor.

But let us not despair, nor be forlorn,
For this is an opportunity,
To shape our own destiny, and be reborn,
And find significance, in our own society.

For in the crafting of our own esteem,
We find the power to transcend,
The limitations of our mortal being,
And find a purpose that is most grand.

Eminence, a product of our own will,
Forged through the fire of life's trials,
A construct of human artifice, still
Through effort, determination, and denial.

But let us not lament nor implore,
For this is an opportunity,
To shape our own destiny, and soar,
And find significance, in our own society.

For in the crafting of our own esteem,
We find the power to transcend,

The limitations of our mortal being,
And find a purpose that is most grand.

So let us seize the reins, and forge ahead,
And in the eminence we create, find true freedom, and spread.

Thus, adorned with self-determined worth and might,
We shall transcend the lamentations of the night.

# 51. Eulogy for a Silenced Melodiousness

The electrocardiogramic emitter forthwith released
Its final harmonious oscillation's tone,
Upon cessation, nary a clap was increased
In sign of commendation, nought was shown.

The metric pulse's rhythm, now stilled and ceased,
No longer did its melodious chime ring,
Silence, the only sound that now was released
In the absence of accolades' sweet sing.

The absence of applause, a sad lament,
For music so melodious and sublime,
But though it may have met with discontent,
Its beauty shall forever in our mind shine.

Though nought was shown in sign of approbation,
The music lives on in our recollection.

For though the electrocardiogramic emitter
released its final oscillations,
the absence of applause, a bitter bitter
does not negate the beauty of its creations.

For true beauty is not in external praise

But in the harmony and melody it conveys,
And though the crowd may not have raised
Their voices in applaud, the music still plays.

In the hearts and minds of those who heard
It will live on, forevermore,
A treasure to be cherished, never blurred
By the lack of outward applause.

So let us not be swayed by accolades,
For true beauty is in the music that never fades.

For music, like the electrocardiogramic emitter,
Releases its final oscillations,
But true beauty, is not just in the meter,
But in the emotions it stimulates and evokes.

For though the crowd may not have shown,
Their appreciation for the final tone,
The music lives on, in the hearts it has flown
And will forever be remembered, not alone.

For true beauty is not in external applause,
But in the feelings it evokes and the cause,
It serves to touch the hearts and souls,
And make our lives, richer and whole.

So let us not be swayed by accolades,
For true beauty is in the music that never fades.

And though the electrocardiogramic emitter
May have released its final oscillations,
Let us not forget the beauty it has offered,
And the emotions it has stirred in our hearts' foundations.

For beauty is not in the accolades,
But in the artistry and craft,
It is not in the applause or the parades,
But in the memories it will always last.

So let us not mourn the absence of claps,
For the music lives on, in our hearts and minds,
It will forever be remembered, in the maps
Of our souls, where beauty forever binds.

For true beauty is not in external validation,
But in the memories and emotions it creates, and the inspiration.

# 52. Eternal Flame: A Sonnet on the Power of Love

On amor, a sentiment most pure and sweet,
That doth the heart with fervor inundate,
A passion that doth make the senses fleet,
And fills the soul with euphoric state.

A force that doth the spirit elevate,
And in its grace, doth all imperfections mar,
A bond that doth the heart's beat synchronize,
And in its splendor, doth the senses star.

But ah, amor's journey oft doth have its woes,
With tears and heartache on its thorny path,
Yet still, in amor's embrace, one ever glows,
And finds the strength to weather any wrath.

Thus, let us love with all our hearts, my dear,
For in its radiance, all else is clear.

For amor is not a fleeting, fickle flame,
But rather, an eternal, burning blaze,
That doth the heart and soul forever claim,
And in its fire, true beauty always stays.

It is the lighthouse that guides us through the night,

And in its light, all doubts and fears take flight,
It is the symphony that gives us insight,
And in its harmony, all wrongs are made right.

So let us cherish amor, and hold it dear,
For in its presence, all else doth pale,
Let us embrace it, and make it ever near,
For in its arms, true felicity shall prevail.

Thus, let us love with all our hearts, my friend,
For in its grace, true amor will never end.

And let us not be afraid to love,
For though it may bring pain and sacrifice,
It is the truest thing that we can do,
And in its light, our souls will rise.

For amor is not a game or a mere sport,
But a sacred thing that should be revered,
It is the most powerful force of all,
That can conquer even death and fear.

So let us open up our hearts and souls,
And let amor in, without any fear,
For in its light, we will find true goals,
And all the beauty that is dear.

Thus, let us love with all our hearts, my dear,
For in its light, we will find true solace and cheer.

And let us not be swayed by societal norms
That dictate what love should be, or how it should be shown
For true amor transcends all forms
And it's the purest thing that we can own.

It's the bond that connects us all,
And it's the thing that makes life worth living
For in amor, we rise above the fall
And find true meaning in the giving.

So let us love with all our hearts and souls
Without fear of judgment or rejection
For amor is the one thing that makes us whole
And gives our lives true direction.

Thus, let us love with all our hearts, my friend
For in its light, true happiness will never end.

And let us not be limited by boundaries,
For true amor knows no borders or divides,
It transcends all races, religions, and cultures,
And in its light, true unity resides.

For love is the one thing that connects us all,
And it's the one thing that makes life worth living.
It brings hope, peace, and happiness to all,
And in its light, true joy is always giving.

So let us love with all our hearts and souls,
Without reservation or hesitation,
For in love, we find true meaning and goals,
And gain true liberation.

Thus, let us love with all our hearts, my dear,
For in its light, true freedom is always near.

And let us not forget, that amor is a journey,
A path that we must constantly travel and explore,
It brings its own set of joys and miseries,
And it's a thing that we must continually adore.

For love is not a destination,
But a process that we must undertake,
It's the one thing that gives our lives sensation,
And the one thing that makes life worth the ache.

So let us embrace the journey of love,
With open arms and hearts, with courage and grace,
For in its light, we will find true peace and above,
And we'll find true beauty in every place.

Thus, let us love with all our hearts, my friend,
For in its light, true life will never end.

# 53. Aevum Luminis : Age of Light

Upon the brink of my ephemeral demise,
Ere my accomplishments and musings reach their zenith,
My heritage, a figment, shall swiftly expire,
And all my aspirations, insipid and effete.

But should the grim reaper's grasp befall me in my prime,
I shall bequeath a plethora of reminiscences,
Of amour and mirth, aspirations and delights supreme,
And all the splendor that existence can proffer.

Though I may not have lived an existence fully fulfilled,
I shall leave behind an indelible impression, a scintillant luminary,
That guides the path for those who chance to encounter,
The same destiny that I did, from nigh or afar.

Therefore let my demise, if it must transpire, be acknowledged,
As naught but a stepping stone to a resplendent daybreak.

And let my name be etched in history's pages,
As one who lived with passion, courage, and grace.

For though my time on earth may be but fleeting,
My legacy, forevermore, shall endure,
A shining beacon for the future's greeting,

A guide for those who seek to be secure.

So let me not be mourned for what I've lost,
But celebrated for all that I have done,
For though my body may return to dust,
My spirit shall live on, forever young.

And when my time on earth has come to end,
I'll leave behind a legacy to befriend,
And guide the ones who follow to ascend,
To greatness, just as I had begun.

And though my mortal coil may be unspun,
My words, my deeds, shall echo on and on,
A symphony of life, forever sung,
A hymn to all that's good and true and strong.

For in this world of pain and sorrow,
I strive to leave a mark, a shining light,
A beacon to guide others to tomorrow,
And show them what it means to live just right.

So let my passing not be seen as loss,
But as a step towards a greater gain,
For though my body may return to moss,
My spirit shall forever remain.

And in the end, when all is said and done,
I'll leave behind a legacy that shines,

A testament to all that I have done,
A legacy of love, of hope, of might.

And though my days upon this earth may cease,
My legacy shall forevermore increase,
A testament to all that I did achieve,
A reflection of the life I did lead.

For in the end, what truly matters most,
Is not the length of time that we have spent,
But how we lived, the seeds that we did sow,
And what we leave behind, as our testament.

So let my passing not be seen as end,
But as a new beginning, a new start,
A chance for others to pick up the pen,
And write their own story with an open heart.

For though my time on earth may be but brief,
My legacy, forevermore, shall be a relief.

# 54. Erudition, the key

Societatis maladies, which do abound,
Bring us to earth with poverty profound,
But there's a way to rise above the fray,
And make a change, starting today.

Erudition, the key, the luminescent guide,
Through darkness, where knowledge doth reside,
Empowering us to break free from oppression,
And end the cycle of inequality's transgression.

From Douglass to Yousafzai, they knew
The power of education to break through,
Their voices raised to inspire change in masses,
To fight for rights and break down classes.

But in this world, education is not equal,
A privilege for some, a sequel for the sequel,
Poverty limits chances to learn, to grow,
And advance, but we must strive to overthrow.

We must fight for education for all,
To break the cycle and answer the call,
For a brighter future, free from oppression,
Where knowledge is the key to true succession.

We must learn from history's lessons well,
And use education as our weapon to dispel
Imperialism and racism, and strive
For a society where equality thrives.

With all our might, let us fight for education,
For a future where poverty is out of sight and
Where imperialism and racism are but a tale,
And true equality and justice shall prevail.

For the children of the future, let us strive,
To make education come alive,
So they may learn to love and care
For their community and the world they share.

To break the chains of poverty and hate,
Education is the key, 'tis fate,
Let us not be complacent, nor delay,
For education is the future, and the only way.

Let us not forget the struggles of the past,
And strive to make education accessible and vast,
For the future of humanity is at stake,
And education is the only way to break the chains.

With eloquence and reason, we must raise our voice,
And fight for education, so that all may rejoice,
In the chance to learn and grow,
For a brighter future, for all to know.

For the world is changing, and 'tis time to take a stand,
For education, for it is the key to a new land,
Where poverty, imperialism, and racism are all gone,
And true equality and justice shall shine on.

So let us strive with all our hearts and souls,
To make education accessible to all,
For in its light, a brighter future unfolds,
Where ignorance and oppression do not enthrall.

# 55. The Veracity Paradox: Navigating a Clouded History

With veracity oft clouded by deceit,
And history writ with political bent,
Whom to believe, and whom to distrust, is meet
With utmost circumspection, lest we repent.

For knowledge learned is oft perverted,
Twisted to serve the ends of those in power,
And truth concealed, till those who are beguiled
Are lost in labyrinths of lies and chatter.

Thus, let us tread with caution in this fray,
And seek the light of truth with diligence,
For in this world of shadows, it doth weigh
Heavy on those who would be in allegiance.

And though the path be fraught with treachery,
Still must we strive for veracity.

And in this quest for veracity,
We must be vigilant and circumspect,
For those who seek to cloud reality
Will use deceit, to hide the truth, to deflect.

But let us not be swayed by their lies,

For truth is like a beacon in the night,
It guides us through the darkness, and the guise
And shines a light on what is wrong or right.

So let us seek the truth with all our might,
And in its light, let us find clarity,
For in a world of deceit and shadows, it's the only light that could guide us truly.
And give us the strength to rise above the treachery.

And let us not forget, that truth is ever-changing,
As our perspectives and understanding evolve.
It may not be the same for all, but still, it's worth pursuing,
For in its light, our souls and minds will solve.

For in the quest for veracity,
We must be willing to question and to learn,
To constantly strive for objectivity
And to discard, what is false or to discern.

And though the path may be fraught with danger,
Let us not falter, in our search for truth,
For in its light, we'll find the strength to conquer
And rise above, the lies and the uncouth.

For truth is the only guide that truly leads,
In a world where deceit and shadows breed.

And so, let us not be swayed by deceit,

But strive for veracity in all we do,
For truth is the only path that we should keep,
And falsehoods, the only thing we should eschew.

For in the quest for truth, we must be bold,
And brave the storms of lies and uncertainty,
For only then, can we be truly told,
What is real and what is mere fantasy.

And though the journey may be long and hard,
Let us not falter, nor lose our way,
For in the end, the truth will be our guard,
And light our path, to a brighter day.

So let us seek the truth with all our might,
And in its light, find the strength to rise above the plight.

So let us be vigilant in our quest,
For veracity, in all we do,
For in a world where deceit is at its best,
The truth is the only thing that's true.

And though the journey may be long and tiring,
Let us not falter, nor lose our way,
For in the end, the truth will be our guiding,
And light our path, to a brighter day.

Let us not be swayed by those who seek to deceive,
But strive for objectivity, in all we see,

For only then, can we truly believe,
And find the truth, that sets us free.


So let us seek the truth with all our might,
And in its light, find the strength to rise above the plight.

# Chapter56

# 57. Eternitatem Veritas : Eternity Truth

Mors, when thou doth knock upon my door,
I'll greet thee with a smile, for I am sure,
That all the battles fought before,
Have made me strong and versatile.

A legacy I'll leave behind,
Of verse that doth like blades entwine,
Of truths that set the mind free,
And lessons for the generations yet to be.

I'll show the world that I was here,
And that my voice still echoes clear,
I'll be remembered through the years,
As rebel and a leader, who did for the voiceless ears.

So when thou doth knock upon my door,
I'll be prepared to make the journey o'er,
For in my heart, I'll always know,
That I lived life with pride and valor, aglow.

Like Immortal Technique, my legacy,
Shall forever in the hearts of men, be.
A voice for the oppressed, a guiding light,
In the fight for freedom, justice and right.

My words, like arrows, shall not miss their mark,
For they are forged in fire and in the dark,
Of oppression and inequality,
But they shall rise, like phoenix, to set the mind free.

Like Petrarca, Spenser, and Shelley,
I'll sing of love and passion, poetry,
But also of the struggles of the poor,
And the injustices that we must endure.

And though death may come to claim my breath,
My words shall live on, long after my death,
For they are not just mine, but of the masses,
The voice of the oppressed, in rhyme and classes.

So let my legacy be one of hope,
And of the power of education to empower and cope,
With the ills of society, let us strive,
For a brighter future, where all can truly thrive.

And let my legacy be one of change,
A catalyst for a world rearranged,
Where poverty, imperialism and racism are no more,
And true equality and justice are the law.

Let my verse be a call to action,
A beacon of hope in times of fraction,
A reminder of the power of education,

To break the chains of oppression and bring liberation.

Let my words be a light in the dark,
Guiding the way for a new spark,
Of hope and change in the world,
For a brighter future for all unfurled.

So if death comes knocking at my door,
I'll greet it with a smile, for I am sure,
That my legacy will live on,
Through the power of education, it will be reborn.

# 58. Vindication Triumph: A Sonnet of Resilience

When rapacious foes did seek to purloin
The riches that by lawful right were mine,
I smiled, for I did clearly foreshadow
That I would reclaim them and malign

The wrongs inflicted, though I lost the fight.
My assurance was unshaken and steadfast,
For though I fell, I knew that I'd attest
The eminence I'd reached, and leave them dry.

Let them believe they've conquered and extol
Their spurious victories o'er my fate,
For I shall return, and all their songs ensnare
In the conflagrations of my own state.

For I am one who knows that I'll transcend
The fray, and claim what's rightfully mine.

With steadfast heart and indomitable will,
I'll rise again and conquer, nay, fulfill
My destiny, and claim my rightful place,
Unchained by doubts, unshackled by disgrace.

Through trials fierce, and battles fierce and long,

I'll forge my strength, and build my power strong,
Until the day that I reclaim my throne
And prove my worth, before the world is shown.

For I am one who knows that I am great,
And I will not be held down by fate,
I'll break the chains that bind me, and create
A new world, free from all that came before.

So let them think they've won, let them believe
That they have conquered, and that I'll not grieve.

For I will rise again, and they shall see
The true power of my sovereignty.

With each step forward, I will leave behind
The doubts and fears that once clouded my mind,
For I am one who knows that I will find
My way to victory, in due time.

Through every storm, I'll stand tall and brave,
And with each passing day, my strength will pave
The path to glory, as I reclaim
My rightful place, and earn my rightful fame.

And when at last, I reach the summit's peak,
I'll look down upon my foes, and speak
The words they longed to hear, but never thought
They'd hear from me, the victor, as I've brought

My kingdom back to life, restored to its prime,
And prove to all, that I am truly sublime.

But let it not be said that I have won
Through malice or through malice and through none,
For I am one who knows that victory
Is not just the defeat of one's adversary.

I'll lead with grace and honor, and with care,
And build a world that's fair and just and square,
A kingdom where the weak and strong alike
Are treated with the same respect and right.

And as I reign, I'll always keep in mind
That power comes with great responsibility,
And I'll use it to better all mankind,
And leave a legacy of humility.

So let my foes and doubters all take note,
For I am one who will not be forgot.

For I am one who knows that I will shine,
And leave a mark that will forever be mine.

And though my rule may one day come to an end,
My name will live on, in tales and legend.
For I am one who knows that true success
Is not in fleeting glory, but in progress.

I'll build a kingdom where the arts and science
Thrive, and knowledge is not met with defiance,
Where every voice is heard, and every soul
Is granted equal opportunity and goal.

And when my reign is over, and my days
Have come to an end, I'll look back in praise,
For all that I have accomplished, and be proud
Of what I've built, and what I've said out loud.

For I am one who knows that I have been
A ruler true, and not a tyrant king.

# 59. Ethereal Adieu: A Sonnet of Farewell to the World

Adieu, dear orb, that oft has been my sanctuary,
Thou art the stage whereon my being was portrayed,
But now the final curtain has been lowered,
And I must depart from thy theater for eternity.

Thou hast been witness to my ecstasies and sorrows,
And beheld my triumphs, and my follies, so humbling,
Thou art the mirror where my psyche was unveiled,
And where my frailties and strengths were manifested.

But now the hour has arrived for me to depart,
And relinquish the experiences I've accumulated,
My tenure here is concluded, I must comprehend.

Though my heart may be heavy, and tears may flow,
I'll bid farewell to thee, and seek solace,
In realms beyond, where veracity and rationality forever glow.

But though my corpus may fade into the abyss,
My essence shall forever endure,
Immortalized in the minds of those I miss,
And in the reverberations of my acts, pure.

For though this mortal coil may be my final rest,

It is but a portal to another plane,
Where my being shall transcend,
And in eternal radiance, forever sustain.

So farewell, dear sphere, my time with thee
Has been a journey fraught with joy and sorrow,
But now it's time for me to bid adieu,
And to the next existence, I must borrow.

Though my departure may bring lament and grief,
I'll carry your love and memories, forever, as a relief.

Though I depart from this terrestrial sphere,
I'll not forget the moments that brought me delight,
The laughter, love, and joy that will forever adhere,
Etched in my heart as my truest and brightest light.

I'll miss the vistas, the aural delights, the fragrances that make
This world so rich, so vivacious, so alive,
But I go forth, with no remorse, no ache,
For I have lived, and truly thrived.

Farewell, dear sphere, my time with thee
Has been a journey fraught with evolution and tribulation,
But now it's time for me to bid adieu,
And embrace the next phase of existence with elation.

Though my departure may bring sorrow and tears,
I'll forever cherish the memories, throughout the years.

# 60. Unspoiled Authenticity: A Sonnet on Being True to Oneself

Inimitable Originality, a virtue recondite,
A condition of being veracious to oneself, unsullied,
Abstain from emulating another's demeanor,
For in genuineness, true might's obfuscated.

Do not accede to societal expectations,
But rather, let thy idiosyncratic self radiate,
For in thine own individuality, true fortitude resides,
And eminence, it shall transpire to thee.

The route to true accomplishment is not to imitate,
But to espouse thyself, in all thy imperfections,
For in singularity, true enchantment
And true satisfaction, it shall be thine motivation.

So be true to thyself, in all thy modus operandi,
And let thine authentic self, forever incandesce.

Let not the opinions of others guide thy path,
But let thy inner voice be thy true guide.
For in authenticity, true power lies,
And in originality, true strength resides.

Do not be swayed by the crowd's demands,
But let thy unique self be thy true guide.
For in thine own identity, true freedom stands,
And true greatness, it shall come to find.

So let not the world dull thy shine,
But let thy authentic self, forever glow.
For in originality, true beauty lies,
And true fulfillment, it shall be thine goal.

So be true to thyself, in all thy ways,
And let thine authentic self, forever blaze.

And let not fear of judgement hold thee back,
But let thy true self, unbridled, take flight.
For in authenticity, true courage lies,
And true wisdom, in originality's sight.

Do not be afraid to march to a different drum,
But let thy unique self, be thy true guide.
For in thine own individuality, true power comes,
And true victory, it shall be thine side.

So let not conformity be thy prison,
But let thy authentic self, forever thrive.
For in originality, true liberation,
And true joy, it shall be thine to arrive.

So be true to thyself, in all thy ways,
And let thine authentic self, forever blaze.

And let not the weight of expectations weigh thee down,
But let thy true self, unencumbered, soar.
For in authenticity, true liberation lies,
And true fulfillment, in originality's core.

Do not be afraid to blaze your own trail,
But let thy unique self, be thy true guide.
For in thine own identity, true success awaits,
And true glory, it shall come to reside.

So let not the world dim thy inner light,
But let thy authentic self, forever shine.
For in originality, true brilliance lies,
And true happiness, it shall forever be thine.

So be true to thyself, in all thy ways,
And let thine authentic self, forever blaze.

And let not the doubts or insecurities hold thee back,
But let thy true self, unshaken, rise above.
For in authenticity, true confidence lies,
And true power, in originality's glove.

Do not be afraid to be different, to stand out,
But let thy unique self, be thy true guide.
For in thine own identity, true victory's about,

And true triumph, it shall come to abide.

So let not the norm be thy cage,
But let thy authentic self, forever break free.
For in originality, true freedom lies,
And true success, it shall forever be.

So be true to thyself, in all thy ways,
And let thine authentic self, forever blaze.

And let not the expectations of others dictate thy fate,
But let thy true self, unbridled, take the lead.
For in authenticity, true leadership lies,
And true inspiration, in originality's seed.

Do not be afraid to chart your own course,
But let thy unique self, be thy true guide.
For in thine own identity, true victory's source,
And true achievement, it shall come to reside.

So let not the mold hold thee back,
But let thy authentic self, forever break free.
For in originality, true innovation lies,
And true success, it shall forever be.

So be true to thyself, in all thy ways,
And let thine authentic self, forever blaze.

# Khublei Shi Hajar Nguh

Thank you, reader, for taking time to read this book,

The story of love and loss, the words we took.

With each turn of the page, your eyes did look,

Into a world of imagination, where we took,

You to a journey, that left you hooked.

 We're grateful for your time, the moments we took,

To share with you, the story of our look,

And now we say, Thank you, our dear reader, book,

For lending us your ear, with every turn of the hook,

And following us to the end, with each chapter, you took.

 Like Bilbo in his journey, with Frodo you took,

A journey of adventure, with each chapter, you look,

And with Sam, you wept, for Frodo's book,

And the ring of power, that left you hooked.

Thank you, reader, for taking time to read this book.

 And like Romeo, in love with fair Juliet, you took,

A journey of passion, with each word, you look,

And with each sonnet, you felt the power of their book,

And the tragedy that came, left you hooked.

Thank you, reader, for taking time to read this book.

 Like Sherlock, in his quest for justice, you took,

A journey of mystery, with each clue, you look,

And with Watson, you solved, each case, with every book,

And the twists and turns, left you hooked.

Thank you, reader, for taking time to read this book.

In gratitude, we say, Thank you, reader, for each look,

That you gave, to this story, and the time you took,

And we hope, that you'll read other books, that we've hooked,

And find the joy, in each page, that you took.

Thank you, reader, for completing this book.

We hope that in the future, you'll take a look,

At other books by the same author, in the store, or online book.

And find the joy, in each story, that we took,

And be hooked, by the words, that we wrote.

Thank you, reader, for reading this book.

Warm regards ,

A - Team

# Note


*As I, a breviloquent raptor, wield A lever, with naught else to my design, I generate tones for the aural field In this prosaic orb we call mankind. My actions, though, are but a small part Of forces far beyond my control, For nature holds the key to each chart And sets the laws that govern the whole. But still, I am compelled to explore The workings of this vast machinery, To seek the truth that lies at core And find the answers to humanity. Though some may call it quest I'll seek the truth, with no time to rest.*

# About The Author

Meet Mawphniang, a man of many parts,
A lawyer, entrepreneur, and more,
With boundless curiosity, and open heart,
And a passion for life, that he will explore.

With talent, drive, and a thirst for success,
He has achieved much, in the professional sphere,
But it is in writing, where he finds the best,
And where his true passion, shines so clear.

With boundless curiosity and verve,
He embraces new ideas, with an open mind,
And ventures boldly, into unknown lands,
With fearlessness, that is truly one of a kind.

From Syadheh Village, in Ri Bhoi District,
He hails, a soul ever-striving, never at rest.
And as he writes his story, with fearlessness,
He makes the most of every moment, ever-unfurled.

And though his journey, may take many roads,
Each step, a step toward self-discovery,
With every word, he shares his soul's abode,
And invites us all, to join in, and be.

For Mawphniang, life is a precious gift,
To be cherished, and explored, with all one's might,
And as he writes, he lifts, our spirits, and uplifts,
With tales of wonder, and delight.

So let us follow, this soul ever-striving,
And be inspired, by his boundless energy,

For Mawphniang, is a man truly thriving,

In a world, that he makes, all the more lovely.

And as we read, his words, so full of life,

We too, shall be, forever, changed by his strife.

And though his journey, may be filled with strife,

He never loses sight, of what is true,

For he knows, that in the end, it is life,

That gives us meaning, and a purpose too.

And so, he writes, with a heart full of love,

And a mind, that is always seeking more,

For he knows, that in the depths, of the dove,

Lies the answers, to life's great riddle, and score.

And as we read, his words, so full of grace,

We too, shall be, forever, touched by his pen,

For Mawphniang, is a man, with a gentle face,

And a heart, that is always, filled with love again.

So let us cherish, this soul ever-striving,

And be inspired, by his boundless energy.

Warm regards ,

A - Team